P9-DTD-819

A Canadian Writer's Pocket Guide

Fifth Edition

Jack Finnbogason
Kwantlen Polytechnic University

Al Valleau
Kwantlen Polytechnic University

1914–2014
Nelson Education celebrates 100 years of Canadian publishing

NELSON EDUCATION
CELEBRATE LIFELONG LEARNING

NELSON EDUCATION

A Canadian Writer's Pocket Guide,
Fifth Edition

by Jack Finnbogason and Al Valleau

**Vice President, Editorial:
Higher Education**
Anne Williams

Executive Editor:
Laura Macleod

Marketing Manager:
Amanda Henry

Developmental Editor:
Lisa Berland

Permissions Coordinator:
David Strand

**Content Production
Manager:**
Claire Horsnell

Copy Editor:
Lisa Laframboise

Proofreader:
Pushpa

Indexer:
BIM Publishing Services

Production Coordinator:
Loretta Lee

Design Director:
Ken Phipps

Interior Design:
Peter Papayanakis

Cover Design and Image:
Johanna Liburd

Compositor:
Cenveo Publisher Services

**Library and Archives
Canada Cataloguing in
Publication**

Finnbogason, Jack, 1942-,
author

   A Canadian writer's
pocket guide / Jack
Finnbogason, Kwantlen
Polytechnic University,
Al Valleau, Kwantlen
Polytechnic University. —
Fifth edition.

Includes bibliographical
references and index.ISBN
978-0-17-653161-4 (pbk.)

   1. English language—
Rhetoric. 2. English
language—Grammar.
I. Valleau, Al, 1946-, autho
II. Title. III. Title: Writer's
pocket guide.

PE1408.F452 2014
808'.042   C2013-904999-1

ISBN 13: 978-0-17-653161-
ISBN 10: 0-17-653161-0

The Writing Process

Over three thousand years ago, Greek thinkers believed that the process of composing (whether in written or spoken form) could best be studied by breaking it down into three stages: invention, disposition (organizing and writing), and style (manner, tone, voice, level of diction, and rhetorical strategies). The comparable stages today are *prewriting, drafting,* and *revising,* and every writer faces the challenge of successfully managing each element in composing an effective paper. We also know now that these activities are actually recursive in that writers perform them simultaneously and repetitively. As a writer, you need to develop and refine the skills and abilities associated with each of these activities to improve your range, competence, and clarity.

1 PREWRITING I: THE BASICS

Typically, when you first sit down to write, it is in response to an assignment, whether it be a report, a review, a summary, or an essay. The basic questions that confront you at the beginning of a writing project are related to five main elements: *purpose, audience, stance, research*, and *outline.*

1-a Purpose

To write well, you have to understand your aim or intention. You need to know if you are writing to inform, persuade, describe, narrate, summarize, define, explain, recommend, or compare. The following guidelines will help you to articulate the purpose of your assignment.

- Read the instructions in the assignment carefully.
- Underline the key verbs in the assignment. (See Chapter 12d for information about verbs you are likely to encounter in assignment instructions.)
- Ask a classmate what he or she thinks the purpose of the assignment is.
- Learn to distinguish the demands of different types of writing. For example, a *report* asks you to identify a problem and make recommendations for

solving it (see Chapter 63 in Web Part XII); a *comparison* asks you to examine two or more topics to find similarities and differences; an *analysis* asks you to examine the elements or parts of a topic and study their relationships.

- Make a rough outline of your intended response to the assignment and ask your instructor for feedback.

1-b Audience

It is important for you to know your audience and how that audience might influence your approach. If you are writing an assignment for a class, your audience will most likely be your instructor. If you are asked to write a report that will be read by a wider audience, you need to ask yourself questions about its members. Will they be informed or unaware? hostile or sympathetic? attentive or easily distracted? A clear understanding of your audience will smooth your progress through the subsequent stages of the writing process and help to ensure that the prose you produce is neither lifeless nor inappropriate in diction and voice.

1-c Stance

Stance is a complex but important part of writing. To understand it fully, you first have to know that your relationship to your audience creates your *voice*, and your relationship to your topic creates your *tone*. How you feel about your topic supplies your tone, while how you see your audience—and, more particularly, how you want that audience to see you—creates your voice. A writer's stance, then, is the combined effect of voice and tone. If you are certain of what your voice and tone should be, you will not have problems with stance.

1-d Research

One of the first questions you must answer in the prewriting stage is whether you need to conduct formal research or whether the information you already possess is adequate. There are a number of prewriting techniques that will help you discover what you already know and feel about your topic. Any research that needs to be done should be well under way before you begin work on the outline of your essay and start a first draft. For information about the research process, see Chapter 14.

1-e Outline

One of the first prewriting techniques most writers learn is outlining, the means by which a writer first defines concretely the theme, parts, and sequence of his or her paper. An outline is a sequenced description, using words, phrases, or sentences, of the paper's thesis and support. An outline is the best way for a writer to capture an initial sense of what the paper will do and how it will do it.

Assume that you have become interested in the stories printed in newspapers about the major changes in the output of natural gas and light oil in Canada and the United States. The introduction of widespread hydraulic fracturing (or "fracking") to revive wells that have been closed and to improve the productivity of new wells has, we are told, made liquid natural gas and light oil abundantly available. You have read enough to know that Canada's gas and oil exports to the U.S.A. are threatened by the introduction of this new technology. You also know there are sources suggesting that this technology will harm the environment.

You do some more research through Google and read sources such as *Wikipedia* and analyses that argue in favour of fracking for the boom in production and other articles opposed because of potential harm to the environment. You have even read several works that suggest it is a technology that has no real future. In short, you feel you have learned enough to be ready to create a *scratch outline*. The following is a possible result:

- the origins of the hydraulic fracturing technology in the 1940s and the first commercial application in 1949

- the fact that the rate of flow in a well declines sharply within one or two years

- the use of fracking to revive the flow of wells that have ceased to be productive and to improve the output of new wells

- the estimation that 60% of new oil and gas wells are using the technology and were already doing so by 2010

- the suspension of this technology in some countries, especially Europe, and even in Quebec

- the reasons for fearing the new technology, including its production of gases and chemicals that can rise back to the surface and possibly affect both surface environments and underground aquifers

- the requirement, in fracking, for many chemical additives, used to increase the flow rate of the gas or oil

- arguments between producers and environmentalists over the effects of fracking

- the struggles of such major players as Chesapeake Energy to make a profit

- reduction of gas prices from $14 per thousand cubic feet of gas in 2005 to $3.88 in 2011

- the increasing financial struggles of companies like Chesapeake because of the need to keep sinking new wells to make profits to pay for the loans they have from major banks

- the announcement by General Electric in late May of 2013 that it will be investing billions of dollars in the shale-fracturing business

You have done enough preliminary checking to decide that you want to do a fuller causal analysis and suggest what the best choice of action might be.

The main thing you have established with the scratch outline is the identification of your purpose. You are not interested in just summarizing the issues involved in the arguments over improved production of an essential commodity and the counterargument about huge environmental costs involved in the means by which the enhanced production is achieved. You want to dig into the differences of opinion on whether fracking is a helpful new technology or not and come to your own position. You also wish to offer backing for that position.

To that end, you should move to a formal outline. A *formal outline* is always a useful planning step when you are writing a paper that has multiple pages and some degree of complexity. This exercise ensures that you have a clear plan of your position and how you want to convey it, while moving from a plan to a finished analysis. A formal outline essentially rehearses your entire analysis with each point representing as much as a paragraph or more. It also attempts to sketch the structure you will use in your analysis. Formal outlines can use words, phrases, or sentences. Generally, they adhere to an established format that has the following general structure:

- *introduction*: includes background and thesis
- *body of essay*: its working paragraphs
- *final position*: a restatement of the thesis as it has been reshaped by the body of the essay

I. Introduction
   A. Background
      1. American application of hydraulic fracturing in 1949; explanation of hydraulic fracturing
      2. Creation of fracking model using chemicals and grit added to water in 1997, leading to 60% of new wells using the model by 2010
      3. Dominance of this model for all American and most Canadian wells
      4. Rapid increase in the output of light oil and liquid natural gas (LNG) in America
   B. Thesis: Although the central debate over fracking's good and bad dimensions has occupied our attention, the real issue is whether this technology has an extended and reliable future or whether it is at best a temporary measure to address the American shortage of gas and oil reserves. If that future is short, then the costs of pursuing it are harder to justify. A final position will be presented in the conclusion.

II. Body of the Essay
   A. Beginnings
      1. The claim by oil/gas companies that 45% of American gas production and 17% of oil production would be lost without hydraulic fracturing
      2. The counterclaims emerging from different sources that threats to the environment, water tables, air quality, and the atmosphere are unavoidable side-effects of fracking

    3. The removal of fracking from regulatory oversight by the EPA (Environmental Protection Agency) in the U.S. and its recent partial reinstatement

    4. Debates in Canada about fracking and about pipeline construction and its effects on environments; Quebec's decision to disallow fracking in a primary area pending further study

B. The debate's mature phase

    1. The industry's insistence that America could never be free of dependence on foreign energy sources without using fracking in all new wells; the corporate prediction that fracking created necessary profits and critical supplies of oil and gas

    2. The industry and government claim that the resources would yield a hundred years of supply using the new technology, a prediction that has become known as the Obama prediction because it was supported by the government

    3. The counterclaim that fracking promotes excessive use of water, the return of chemicals and polluted water to the surface, mishandling of waste, increased methane levels in the atmosphere, and residues from the acids used in the process

    4. The counterclaim that this source of oil and gas has, at best, a life of 11–25 years before running out of shale resources to work on, a direct attack on the Obama prediction

    5. The increasing difficulty of making a profit since production costs are outstripping market returns; the declaration of bankruptcy by some of the companies

C. The most likely end to the debate

    1. Economic analysis shows that fracking is increasingly not commercially viable, e.g., Chesapeake

Energy's difficulty in making a profit. Companies have to keep drilling new wells and using fracking to make money to pay the interest on their loans; Chesapeake Energy, the largest company involved, has $11 billion of cumulative debt.

2. The North American price for LNG fell from $14 per 1000 cubic feet in 2007 to $3.50 in 2013. The European price is closer to $12 per 1000 cubic feet.

3. LNG and light oil dissipate quickly even with the fracking technology, so companies must constantly drill new wells. Companies are now adjusting their valuation of their reserves and potential profits because of the expense involved in this drilling.

4. Reliable analysts say that LNG is more costly to harvest than the current market price. The rapid increase of supplies of light oil and LNG produced by this technology in places like the U.S.A. and Canada led immediately to a decline in prices because of the abundant supply.

5. The March 2–8, 2013, edition of *The Economist* points out that the American price per million British Thermal Units is $3.40 and the European price is $12; yet American producers have not even begun to export their product. *The Economist* argues they should be exporting LNG, not importing it, simply for fiscal reasons.

III. Final Position: The debate between the corporate producers of liquid natural gas and light oil from shale sources and the environmentalists will continue. At present, it is focused on the relative benefits of, on the one hand, having a reliable energy resource because of the hydraulic fracturing technology and the large drilling program, and, on the other, having cleaner air, larger aquifers, no leakage and backflow of chemicals and refuse, and a cleaner atmosphere. Both parties to the debate may be missing the more central point. The companies producing this resource cannot continue to do so economically. Since the normal application of supply and demand forces will continue to keep the prices low, this is an industry running out of time. *The Economist's* suggestion that American and Canadian producers should be shipping to markets where the product is worth three times its North American value may need to be studied and implemented. If it is not, it will not matter how much potential supply exists because its production costs are higher than its market value.

PREWRITING II: TECHNIQUES 2

During the prewriting stage, you can explore the topic you wish to write about by using one or more of the following techniques: *brainstorming, mind-mapping, freewriting and looping, branching, the pentad,* or *topic analysis.*

2-a Brainstorming

Brainstorming is an exercise in free association that involves listing your responses to a topic. As you perform this activity, do not pause to reflect on organizational considerations, such as the order of the ideas and the relationships between the ideas. Simply list as quickly as possible all the ideas and associations that come to you.

2-b Mind-Mapping

Mind-mapping involves creating a *visual representation* of the relationships among ideas. To create a mind-map, take a blank sheet of paper and write your topic in the centre of the page. Draw a circle around the topic. Then write down the major ideas associated with the topic, circle each idea, and draw lines connecting the ideas to the topic in the centre. Next, write down minor ideas that relate to the major ideas, circle the minor ideas, and connect them to the main ideas. If even more specific ideas occur to you, record those ideas and connect them to the minor ideas. Continue this process until you run out of ideas.

2-c Freewriting and Looping

Freewriting is simple. Set a time limit of five minutes or so and write continuously about the topic, never letting your pen stop. If you cannot think of any ideas, keep writing *thinking* or *can't write* until something does come to mind.

Looping is a more directed form of freewriting. Imagine that you are writing an essay on Louis Riel. You may not know what position you want to take even though you have done some preliminary reading. Looping is an ideal method for exploring how you feel about a topic. First, produce a statement (e.g., "When I think about Louis Riel, I think . . .") and spend five minutes freewriting about that statement. Next, read what you have written and isolate one sentence, image, or phrase that surprises you the most. Use this unexpected element as your starting point for another five minutes of freewriting. Continue this process until you reach a point of diminishing returns.

2-d Branching

Branching is a variation on mind-mapping. The chief difference is that branching proceeds in a much more linear way. The first step in branching is to break your topic down into as many parts as suggest themselves to you. If your analysis were to produce five topic parts, you would be left with five branches to explore. To the right of each branch, you would add new branches consisting of supporting ideas.

Branching gives you a better understanding of how the constituent parts of your topic relate to one another. It also gives you a clearer sense of any gaps in your knowledge of the topic, thereby allowing you to identify areas in which you need to do more research.

2-e The Pentad

The pentad[1] is a set of five headings that helps you to discover, classify, and organize the relationships among the main parts of your topic. This prewriting technique emerged in part from the work of the American literary critic Kenneth Burke and in part from the traditional questions of journalism—*who, what, when, where, how,* and *why.* The pentad, which is based on Burke's five terms (listed below), is a useful mechanism for generating additional details when you are writing an essay about people and/or events.

TERM	DEFINITION	ACTION
ACT	the "what" of an event	the central act, what happened
SCENE	the "when" and "where"	the background of an event, including the physical space and the time in which the act occurred; includes the culture of a place and time
AGENT	the "who"	the person or persons or key force involved in the central event
AGENCY	the "how"	the means by which the act or event was accomplished
PURPOSE	the "why"	the intended objective or end; the reason the act was committed or the event occurred; the purported aim of the action

Listed below are the ten possible pairings (or *ratios,* as Burke calls them) you can use to explore a topic that involves actions or people:

Act–Scene   Scene–Agent   Agent–Agency   Agency–Purpose
Act–Agent   Scene–Agency   Agent–Purpose
Act–Agency   Scene–Purpose
Act–Purpose

Burke's ratios allow you to examine in a systematic fashion the relationships among the main parts of your topic. For example, *Act–Purpose* forces you to answer central questions about the event and its intent, while *Act–Agent* yields

---

[1] This section adapted from W. Ross Winterowd, ed., *Contemporary Rhetoric: A Conceptual Background with Readings* (New York: Harcourt Brace Jovanovich, 1975), 155–62.

useful connections between the event and the person or force that caused the event. By analyzing these and other ratios, you may generate additional details as well.

2-f Topic Analysis

Called *topoi* (topics) by the Greeks, topic analysis is a prewriting technique that involves using a set list of questions to generate details about your topic. The activities associated with topic analysis (comparing, contrasting, defining, classifying, and so forth) require you to examine your topic carefully. The sample topic analysis questions that follow are adapted from a list prepared by the American rhetorician Richard Larson.[2]

Exploring a single item

- What are its physical characteristics?
- From what perspectives can it be examined?
- What is its structure?
- How are its parts put together?
- To what class does it belong?
- What uses does it have?
- Who uses it?
- Who or what produced it?

Exploring an event or process

- What happened? (Be precise.)
- What circumstances surrounded this event or process?
- What were its causes?
- What were its consequences?
- Who or what was affected by it?
- What class of events or processes does it belong to?
- Is it good or bad, desirable or undesirable? By whose standards?
- How do you know about it? How reliable is your information?
- To what other events is it connected?

---

[2] Adapted from W. Ross Winterowd, ed., *Contemporary Rhetoric: A Conceptual Background with Readings* (New York: Harcourt Brace Jovanovich, 1975), 144–54.

Writing about abstract concepts (such as socialism or capitalism)

- To what items, group of items, events, or group of events does the word connect?
- What characteristics must an item or event have before this name can be applied to it?
- How do the characteristics of this item or event differ from those of other items or events included in the same class?
- How has the term been used by writers you have read? How have they defined it?
- Do you feel positive toward the item or event named by this term? Negative? What standard inclines you to feel this way?

PREWRITING III: SKILL DEVELOPMENT 3

3-a Reading Skills

Use the following questions to help you become a critical reader:

- What is the writer's purpose?
- Does the writer have a concealed purpose or unannounced bias?
- What do you think the writer's key assumptions are?
- Is any pertinent information ignored?
- Does the point of view distort the material?
- Is the material current?
- Has the writer acknowledged any opposing views and dealt with them?
- Are there any logical problems with the material?
- Does the author expect you to know anything about his or her topic? Do you?
- How does what you know about the topic differ from the information the author presents?

- Does the author support his or her opinions with evidence? Is the evidence convincing? Is it current?
- Is the author an expert in the field? If not, what does he or she know about the field?
- Is the material based on *primary evidence* (the evidence of the author) or on *secondary evidence* (the evidence of others)? If the latter, are the "others" experts in the field?

Techniques such as *previewing, skimming and scanning, highlighting*, and *note-taking* provide concrete assistance as you engage in the reading process.

PREVIEWING

Before you read a book or an article, you should preview it. Previewing ranges from looking through the table of contents or index of a book to scanning the headings and illustrations of an article. Previewing helps you to separate essential information from nonessential information.

SKIMMING AND SCANNING

Skimming and scanning a text go hand in hand with previewing. Whereas previewing a text focuses on particular items, such as a book's index, table of contents, and headings, *skimming* lets you move through the text by reading the first sentence of a passage and quickly assessing the passage's content. You do not read every sentence when you skim a passage; you simply focus on phrases and important terms to arrive at a quick picture of what is in the passage. If you think the passage is of value, you eventually go back and read it carefully. *Scanning* a passage has the same effect. In scanning, you use your finger, a ruler, or a mouse cursor to guide your eyes down the centre of the page. When you do this, you are not reading individual words; rather, you are gaining a quick impression of the content of each line of print.

HIGHLIGHTING

Highlighting or underlining by means of a highlighter or a pen is an effective way to show the important points in a passage.

Another form of highlighting is the marginal note. Marginal notes identify the main idea of each paragraph in the passage. Appended to some of the marginal notes are asterisks, which indicate the relative importance of the paragraph; the greater the number of asterisks, the greater the paragraph's importance. Marginal notes therefore allow you to track the writer's analysis and respond critically to elements in that analysis.

NOTE-TAKING

Although most students have learned to take notes from a classroom overhead, a blackboard or greenboard, or a slide presentation, fewer have mastered efficient note-taking from a speaker, an oral presentation, or a discussion. The same challenge occurs when students are taking notes on highlighted material, trying to make notes that are both brief and sufficient. When actually taking your notes, consider the following factors:

1. *Are the notes connected to a text?* If so, be sure to make a record of the author, the book/article/essay title, the library information, URL or DOI if supplied, and the page or paragraph number of the text. You should record whatever information will be necessary to write a bibliographic reference if you use the material in an essay. In addition, ask yourself the following questions:

    *   Are there any definitions or facts I should record?
    *   Does the material cover what I thought it would, or does it cover ground I was not expecting to cover?
    *   Is there anything in the material I do not understand?
    *   Do my notes cover the material? Can I cover it in a different way?

2. *Are the notes connected to group discussions or lectures?* If so, ask yourself the following questions:

    *   What is the topic of the discussion?
    *   Am I responding to a set of discussion questions?
    *   What have I highlighted as the main ideas?
    *   Are there any cross-references to a text from the discussion or lecture? (If there are, note the page references and highlight the passages the discussion focused on.)

3. *Are the notes intended as primary work for an assignment?* If so, and if that assignment is an essay longer than four pages, you should set up a separate folder for that assignment. Then each set of notes you take on your resource reading can be stored in separate files in that folder. For more information about the note-taking process, see 15-b and Chapter 16.

3-b Listening Skills

Listening skills are as important as reading skills. Here are a few questions you can ask yourself to judge whether you are a good listener, an active listener, and a critical listener:

- What is the main idea the speaker is presenting?
- Are there any supporting facts I should be taking note of?
- Can I predict what the speaker is going to say next or how he or she is going to conclude?
- Do I have any questions about the material? If so, what are they?
- Can I apply the material the speaker is presenting to other material I know?
- Is there any material I disagree with? Why do I disagree with it?

3-c Critical Thinking Skills

Critical thinking skills include *inference, causal analysis, summary, analysis, evaluation, synthesis,* and *the Toulmin model.*

INFERENCE

An inference is the reasoned product of two or more facts. It is one of the most basic mental operations you perform in moving from fact to premise, and it is the core of what you do when you use the Toulmin model. If you know that the Canadian lumber industry had an outstanding period in 2012–2013, what inference might you draw about the American housing market during that same period? You also need to check whether the logic that allows you to make an inference is self-evident or whether you need to explain it in some detail.

CAUSAL ANALYSIS

There are two key elements you need to learn. The first is the ability to discriminate among contributory, necessary, and sufficient causes. A *contributory cause*, as its name implies, is one that assists in the creation of an effect but is not sufficient by itself to produce that effect. A *necessary cause* is one that must be present if an effect is to result but is not by itself sufficient to produce that effect. A *sufficient cause* is the cause or causes that, alone or working together, will ensure that a certain effect is the result. A primary objective of causal analysis is to identify the sufficient cause.

The second key element is to learn to distinguish among *immediate* causes, *intermediate* causes, and *remote* causes. These three terms refer to how close in time a cause is to an effect. You need to discipline yourself to list all the causes you can think of with these three headings as your organizing tool. You will be surprised how often a remote cause turns out to be more important than an immediate cause. The earth tremors that are part of an earthquake, for instance, are not as important to that effect as are shifting plates, a decidedly remoter cause.

SUMMARY

Summarizing is an essential skill for first- and second-year students. Its first purpose is to test your critical reading skills, because it requires you to present the essential matter from a text in your own words in a quarter to a third of the space occupied by that original text. A successful summary therefore retains all the essential matter from a text and filters it through your own language. This filtering action clearly displays the exactness of your understanding of the text being summarized, and this overall process allows you to absorb, reflect on, and present the core meaning of that text.

For a more detailed account of the elements involved in writing a summary, see Chapter 8.

ANALYSIS

Analyzing means "taking apart." This process involves a three-step approach.

1. Divide the topic you are analyzing into its constituent parts.

2. Study the individual parts to see what each contributes to the whole.

3. Reassemble the parts into the whole, commenting on the connections between the parts and the whole.

EVALUATION

An evaluation states why something has, or does not have, value. You have to demonstrate, as concretely as possible, some grounds that support your claim or thesis. Here are four basic steps you should follow in writing an evaluation:

1. State your claim.

2. Present criteria to provide an objective test of your claim.

3. Apply the criteria carefully and thoroughly.

4. Restate your claim but now as a proven rather than merely asserted claim.

SYNTHESIS

Synthesis is the reverse of analysis. To synthesize, you must put things together rather than take them apart. A typical synthesis involves assembling and presenting the views of three or more informed people on a particular topic. A critical synthesis requires you to do more than point out areas of agreement and disagreement among your sources; you must also indicate which view(s) you support and why.

THE TOULMIN MODEL

See 7-b for a description of the Toulmin model.

DRAFTING 4

A clear understanding of the conditions in which you write will help to smooth your progress through this challenging stage of the writing process.

4-a Writing Preferences

Some writers are happiest writing quickly. Others tend to be more reflective and build their work slowly. It is important to understand and work according to your own idiosyncrasies and preferences as a writer. If you are most comfortable writing one part of your draft at a time, then do so. If you prefer to complete your first draft at a single sitting, then feel free to use that strategy.

4-b The Importance of Routine

You should establish a routine for drafting. Routine includes the order in which you do tasks. Whereas some writers like to begin with an easy task and thereby build confidence, others prefer to attack the most challenging tasks first. Ritual also has to do with where you work, when you work, and what kind of atmosphere you work in. There is no right way or wrong way to write, but consistency is important. Establish a routine that suits you, and stick to it.

REVISING 5

Once you have completed your first draft, set it aside for a few days. When you revisit your draft, you should do so with a more critical eye. Your editing will be more effective if you focus on one facet of your draft at a time. Four editing activities that will help you do this are the *structure sweep*, the *development sweep*, the *special-paragraphs sweep*, and the *proofreading sweep*. (For further information on proofreading, see Chapter 18.)

5-a Structure Sweep

The most efficient way to start revising your first draft is to do a structure sweep. When conducting this kind of editing sweep, ask yourself the following questions about the draft:

- Does each paragraph relate clearly to the preceding paragraph and to the following paragraph?
- Does each paragraph have a focus and a purpose?
- Does each paragraph connect to and advance my thesis?
- Is my argument balanced? Are all of its parts equally developed?

5-b Development Sweep

The goal of a development sweep is to verify that the ideas in your draft are supported sufficiently. Using a pen, a highlighter, or your computer's highlighting feature, identify the sentences that define, illustrate, or otherwise support the main ideas you selected during the structure sweep. If your underlining or highlighting in a particular paragraph yields only one or two supporting sentences, that paragraph's main idea is probably not adequately supported.

5-c Special-Paragraphs Sweep

The focus of a special-paragraphs sweep is the introduction, the conclusion, and any other special paragraphs you have written. To begin your special-paragraphs sweep, ask yourself the following questions about the introduction:

- Does it capture the reader's attention?
- Does it clearly establish my claim (thesis)?
- Does it define difficult or challenging terms?
- Does it provide the background necessary to a successful argument?

Next, respond to the following questions about the conclusion:

- Does it restate my claim?
- Does it summarize the main points supporting my argument?
- Does it reiterate the general significance of my topic?
- Does the last sentence express an appropriate note of finality?

5-d Proofreading Sweep

The purpose of a proofreading sweep is to eliminate errors in usage, spelling, and punctuation. Here are some guidelines to assist you with the process:

- Read your essay aloud. Some errors or omissions become more obvious when you hear them.
- After obtaining your instructor's approval, have a fellow student proofread your essay.

- Set your draft aside for a few days and then return to it. Gaining distance from your essay generally leaves you in a better position to spot errors.

- Use former graded assignments and the Correction Abbreviations chart inside the back cover of this book to determine what your most common errors are. Use your awareness of these errors to make your proofreading sweep more efficient.

- Ensure there are no formatting or documentation errors.

Academic Writing

6 PLAGIARISM

6-a Definition

According to the *MLA Handbook for Writers of Research Papers,* seventh edition, the term *plagiarism* derives from a Latin word that means "a kidnapper." It is the writer's kidnapping of someone else's work and the offering of that work as his or her own that is the fundamental element in all cases of plagiarism. This kidnapping is both a theft of another person's work and an intended deception of the paper's audience into believing the work is the writer's. This double act, therefore, explains why the academic community takes cases of plagiarism so seriously.

6-b Practical Examples of Plagiarism

The following represent examples of plagiarism. Each of these examples has actually occurred and represents one form of confusion about what constitutes plagiarism.

a) *But I didn't plagiarize; I just gave my paper to my study partner.*

It does constitute plagiarism in most institutions if an instructor discovers a paper essentially copied, in whole or in part, from another submitted paper. The circumstance is analogous to a student in an exam cheating by looking at another student's exam with that student's compliance. You should know that the penalty for plagiarism in this case is applied to both students and not just to the student who actually copied the paper.

b) *I was just using notes I had borrowed; how was I to know the notes weren't the original work of the student who lent them to me?*

Again, this is an act of plagiarism whether you knew the notes were paraphrases of someone else's work or not. In this case, however, the student who loaned the notes is not guilty of plagiarism.

c) *This data was on the Web; as such, it was in the public domain or common knowledge. So my use of it can't be plagiarism.*

Wrong. Specific data is rarely common knowledge. You would have to show multiple instances of the data being published in accessible sources, such as newspapers or mass circulation magazines, for your defence to be acceptable. Whenever you use specific data from a source in a paper, cite that source.

d) *I have had help from tutors before, including fixing up my sentences and suggesting better wording.*

This still constitutes plagiarism, from the root definition of "using someone else's work without acknowledging your source." A tutor should know better than to do your writing for you, but, if this does occur, you need to acknowledge the assistance. Better still, to avoid unpleasant repercussions, you should ask your instructor what editing help, if any, a tutor can give you. Some institutions forbid such help.

e) *Come on; I only used a couple of phrases on my second page and a sentence or two later. The rest is all my work. So it's ridiculous to call this a plagiarized paper.*

It doesn't matter how much plagiarism occurs. It only matters that you have plagiarized. There is no ascending scale of penalties, with higher deductions as the proportion of plagiarism increases. One sentence, or even just a phrase, is enough to earn the penalty. Cite the source and avoid that penalty.

f) *But I never used the original wording; I was just copying from my notes, and you can see that I used my own wording when making those notes.*

Again, that doesn't matter. The act of plagiarizing is the act of offering someone else's work as your own. If you use the structure of the person's analysis or the same examples in the argument or the same sequence of points, it doesn't matter that you substituted your own words. The same principle applies when you borrow someone else's statistics or data.

g) *I am not guilty of plagiarism. Look in my bibliography; I included the titles of the two works that I used as resources in the actual writing of my paper. So I have attributed my sources; I just did it a little differently than the way you are talking about.*

It's still plagiarism. The fact is that you have to cite each borrowing, whether a direct quotation or a summary or a paraphrase. It may even be only borrowed data that you are acknowledging a source for. If there's no citation of the borrowing at the point it occurs, you are committing plagiarism and are relying on your instructor either not to notice what you have done or to allow you a chance to re-submit the paper with appropriate citations. In most cases, that will not happen.

What does not need to be cited as borrowed material?

1. Obviously, the first answer is your own insights and understanding, expressed in your own words. The only difficulty arises when you think an original position you held has been significantly modified by your reading; at that point, you may have to include a general acknowledgment of your principal influence or influences.

2. You also do not need to include a citation for anything that can legitimately be described as common knowledge or information within the public domain. If something has appeared in multiple public sources, such as newspapers and magazines, then it is common knowledge. Some authorities suggest a minimum of three publicly accessible sources, but your common sense will assist you on this issue.

What do I have to cite in a note or a parenthetic reference?

1. Ideally, you have maintained your notes for your essay in such a manner that you can quickly distinguish a quotation from another form of note. You should, in your notes, use quotation marks and a distinct colour of highlighter to denote direct borrowings from your readings. Remember, each quotation has to be formally acknowledged by quotation marks or segregation from your

text by indenting and a note or parenthetic reference.

2. You must also acknowledge, in citations, all paraphrases and summaries you have included in your paper.

3. Include any help you obtained from a fellow student or a tutor at a learning centre, or any other information that you cannot fairly describe as part of your common knowledge. Write your citation in such a way as to reflect fairly the source of your borrowing.

4. Provide a citation for materials gathered from factual sources, encyclopedias, and specialized dictionaries, whether in paper or electronic formats.

5. Formally acknowledge all materials you used from your online sources. Before deciding what your online sources will be, review the advice about assessing online sources in 14-c.

WRITING THE ACADEMIC ESSAY   7

The experience you gained in high school with papers is useful for the research protocols, planning skills, and organizational experience you learned in dealing with more extended essays. Sometimes, however, students get the sense that a research assignment is an "encyclopedia essay," where the task is chiefly to take information from one place and transfer it, slightly modified, to another. Academic essays, however, expect you to use your research to supplement the knowledge you already have and to support your own perspective.

7-a An Overview

A good place to start in understanding the expectations of academic essay assignments is the purpose of the essay. Generally, you will find three leading purposes.

INFORMATION ESSAY

The first, and possibly the simplest, purpose you will encounter is the "information" essay. It may be a review of the literature in a specific area. Your political science instructor might ask you to explain the changes made by the federal Conservatives in the past four years to equalization payments made to the provinces. The "information" essay has the common purpose of asking you to research a focused subject and summarize what you learned.

ANALYTICAL ESSAY

This assignment requires you to invent your own analytical framework and methods, and that is one of its most challenging features. Analysis is the art of deconstructing a subject, understanding the parts of that subject, and understanding how those parts interact. An English instructor may ask you to analyze two of Keats's odes, stressing their common features and themes. A psychology class may require an analysis of the Stanford prison experiment and what it tells us about how we depersonalize a human subject. You will often find that the subject you are given is asking for more than simple analysis. The psychology example above shows that. Nevertheless, many of the essay choices you will encounter have an analytic purpose.

ARGUMENT ESSAY

A third kind of purpose is signalled directly with words such as "agree or disagree and discuss." However, even an assignment in an American history course asking you to discuss whether the Civil War originated chiefly from social, economic, or political causes is essentially an argument. Many writers find it easier to write from an argumentative edge; you should, of course, get your instructor's agreement for such a shift.

Breaking all your assignments into three purposes involves some simplification. A business class may assign you a statistical topic, but even that will involve some analysis. It is always helpful to make sure you understand the purpose of a writing assignment and what is involved in fulfilling that purpose.

7-b Academic Argument

In postsecondary institutions, essays are a standard means of evaluating students in the humanities and social sciences.

The three most common kinds of assigned topics for essays are **information, analysis/inquiry,** and **argument** topics.

Perhaps the most frequent demand you will face is to research a subject and take a **position** on an issue or issues within it. Argument essays can range from a causal analysis in history to a critique of a major theme in a literary work. In the social sciences, essays in psychology and sociology frequently ask you to evaluate the principal features of a subject and choose a position regarding one of those features. Social sciences essays also ask you to support a reading of data compiled from a survey or questionnaire.

KINDS OF ARGUMENT

There are three kinds of arguments we can construct: arguments of **fact, value,** and **policy.** The argument of **fact** addresses questions of how something happened, what causes precipitated an event, how a subject is constituted, what the subject relates to or influences, and so on. When you are stating the major published goals of Obama's second term in office or the reasons why the Canadian government was supporting oil sands development while aligning its stance on climate change sector by sector with the American stance, you are writing an argument about **fact.** This is also true if you are writing an assessment of human dreaming or of the excesses caused by our multicultural policies.

The argument of **value** specifically addresses the value of your subject, its worth according to the criteria you adopt and apply. The key to a successful argument here is to create sufficient **criteria** and apply them rigorously to make your position persuasive. If you wished to argue that *Silver Linings Playbook* deserved the Academy Award for best film of 2012, you would need to include more criteria than the fact that it is a romantic comedy, a genre much overlooked by the Academy, or that it makes a statement on the complex nature of social dysfunction. Your criteria have to include the elements you believe made the film worthy of the award, including cinematic and thematic values.

The argument of **policy** directly addresses the question of what we should do in response to a problem or an issue (the subject). As you know, elections are, in part, arguments of policy, especially when it comes to matters of finance, environmental decline, health delivery, and foreign policy. In building a policy argument, you have to clarify why some choices are wrong and others are right.

You must also offer reasoned, fact-based arguments for your position in favour of a specific choice of action.

Take, as a single example of how these different forms of argument apply, the health arrangements wherever a provincial government is moving from a local to a more general model of health care delivery.

- An argument of **fact** might ask where a regional model of health delivery came from and how its delivery model differs from the previous arrangement of hospitals having individual budgets assigned by a provincial authority.

- An argument of **value** might examine the positions Canadians hold about the best way of guaranteeing universal public access to health care and argue for one of those positions as having the highest worth. This could, in turn, be applied to the different delivery models.

- A **policy** argument might argue for infusing some degree of private health care into the public model as a means of controlling costs. This argument would necessarily involve you in the debate about universal public health care and how it should be managed.

THE CLASSICAL MODEL OF ARGUMENT

One of the first models of argument that we can learn from is the **classical** or **ancient** model, seen as having either a five-part or a seven-part structure. What we should primarily learn from this model is the importance of establishing the **background** and context of an argument first before entering the **body** or content part.

The Greeks believed that the argument's beginning had three necessary parts, with the first being the **background** to or **context** of the argument.

- In presenting the context, you accomplish the necessary task of **clarifying** for your reader the events or circumstances behind the debate. If we return to our earlier example of the argument in Canada over the delivery of health care, we would begin by sketching how we moved in the 1940s and 1950s from a user-pay model to an insurance-driven model predicated on the belief that all citizens, no matter their age or financial condition, have an equal right to care. We might have to go right back to the first Saskatchewan form of this model in describing the background of the traditional delivery model. We would also need to describe how there began to be trouble funding that model successfully in the last quarter of the twentieth century and why debates arose over alternative delivery models.

- We would next sketch the major **positions** taken on the issues of adequate funding and successful delivery of health care in the past decade. The ancients would insist on this background as an essential prelude to the writer's announcing a particular position.

- Finally, with background established and major positions identified, the reader would be ready for the position you will be supporting. The **major claim** and a **preview** of the argument would be the third element in a classical argument.

The opening of an argument in the classical style would therefore have three distinct parts, answering three distinct questions:

1. What are the **background details** or context of this argument?

2. What **positions** have arisen with respect to the issue/argument?

3. What **thesis** are we going to take and how do we intend to support that thesis?

These opening parts would be followed by the **body** of our argument, which would require your mounting both a "**confirmation**," or "argument for," and a "**refutation**" or "argument against." The arguments for the central claim or thesis always dominate; they are, in turn, built upon individual claims that logically support the main position.

The Greek and Roman orators and writers knew that a complete argument had to directly address the **position of the opposing side** also. In fact, what they called the appeal to ethos (the integrity of the writer) demanded a fair recitation of the opposing position. The successful argument might even make concessions to the counter-argument, since it is rare that a position has no merit. Generally, in writing (or speaking) a refutation, the ancients would first state objectively the opposing position and then suggest reasons why there were problems in maintaining such a position.

It is common for writers to neglect the importance of **refutations**. However, an argument is incomplete without paying attention to the other side. It is simply good practice to do so, but it must be managed in a way that does not give too much prominence to the counterargument. Frequently, that can be accomplished by dealing with it first in the body of the argument and then moving directly into paragraphs of **confirmation**.

In the classical model, the argument's conclusion has two central tasks, to **summarize** and to **restate**. Simply repeating what you have already said in multiple paragraphs will not hold your reader's attention. You need to select the key claims upon which your position rests and find new language to repeat them. In concluding, you also need to focus on your **central claim;** unless you have a **policy** or **action** to recommend, your thesis is normally your last sentence. Some writers like to end by suggesting the general **importance** of the issue being addressed.

We are unlikely to follow the classical model of argument exactly in our academic arguments. However, this model reminds us, with its seven (or five) parts, what the tasks of a successful argument are:

1. Do not normally plunge into the **central claim** of the argument; instead, first establish the **context** of the argument, the domain in which it exists.

2. Include a **narration of the facts**, a full backgrounding of the issue that you are about to take a position on. This both establishes context and gives you a chance to select what you believe the most important facts are. A narration of the facts also allows you to begin in a relatively **neutral** domain.

3. Once the context and background are established, give a full statement of the thesis, the **central claim**, which is the natural bridge into the body of the argument. If the argument is a longer one, you may also wish to follow with a **preview** of the argument's claims as part of the thesis paragraph.

4. Include **counterarguments** as well as **positive arguments** in the body of the essay. As such, there are at least two parts to the body, the essay's longest unit. Remember that the counterargu-

ment should never obscure or receive emphasis equal to the emphasis on the positive argument.

5. Focus the ending on the argument's position. **Summary** naturally precedes the repetition of the **central claim**, but it is the claim that should receive the principal emphasis. Finally, you may also want to suggest an **action or actions** that may be taken if your argument is an argument of **policy**.

ARGUMENT AND ITS APPEALS

An argument has a beginning, a middle, and an end, as we can see when we examine the classical model of argument. Arguments also employ different kinds of appeals. We should remember that the root meaning inherent in the word *argument* is "to move the audience from one position towards another."

The ancient terms for the basic appeals the writer can make are *pathos, logos,* and *ethos*—the appeal to **emotion**, the appeal to **logic**, and the appeal to **integrity**.

- We expect the appeal to *logos*, or **reason/logic**, to dominate our arguments in an academic environment. As such, we build our paragraphs around claims, data, and warrant (using the Toulmin model), or claims based on inductive or deductive logic (using the more traditional terms). We also use expert witnesses, sampling, survey, and other reason-based means to support the claims underpinning our position.

- We should know, however, that argument often includes **appeals to our feelings** and to our **trust in the speaker/writer**. Political campaigns or magazine ads are excellent venues for the appeal to *pathos*, since both political parties and advertisers know that it is easier to motivate us through our emotions than through our mind. A quick survey of ads for cars or clothes or cameras will remind us that sellers want to get to our desires, not to our mental capacities. You may wish to include an appeal to emotion; however, academic argument values claims supported by facts, data, and reasoning, so that appeal must be dominant.

- The appeal to *ethos*, or the "good person" argument, is subtler, but it essentially involves speakers/writers asking us to believe them because they are honest and have our best interest at heart. In an argument, when we concede a good point to the other side of the issue, we may also be appealing to ethos because such a concession reinforces in the reader a sense of our **fair-mindedness**. Equally, when we take the time to provide a full background for the issue we are examining before we state our position, we leave an impression of impartiality. Generally, writing that relies on reasoned positions rather than slanting or absolute statements is more likely to create an appeal to ethos and give the general sense of a fair-minded writer/speaker who can be trusted.

INDUCTIVE AND DEDUCTIVE REASONING

The earliest means of appealing to logos was through what came to be called **inductive** and **deductive** reasoning. **Inductive reasoning** began with particular examples and attempted to use them to support a generalization. Individual examples were analyzed to discover a pattern, and the pattern, once discovered and supported, provided a basis for the generalization.

In the current argument for global warming, for instance, scientists compare the average warming effect of the past two or three decades with the fluctuation of temperatures over a similar period earlier in the twentieth century. The difference between these two periods is then used to support the generalization that the Earth is getting warmer. Even the more limited use of data based on the annual shrinkage of glaciers in the extreme north or south is an instance of inductive reasoning: one would examine the particular instances, discover the pattern in these particulars, and articulate the general claim that the particulars support. Even the movement of polar bears away from a traditional habitat can become a meaningful particular supporting the global warming generalization.

The strength of an inductive argument lies in the **comprehensiveness** and **representative** nature of the examples it employs to support its claim or claims. The tests you need to apply to your examples include the following questions:

1. Are my examples representative rather than specialized?

2. Are my examples sufficient to support my claim?

3. Are my examples random ones rather than specially selected ones?

4. Are my examples typical and various? (Ideally, your examples should show some variety.)

5. Does my claim go beyond the boundaries covered by my examples?

6. Do my examples contain reasonable predictive force?

Deductive reasoning, in its earliest form, attempts to replace experience with logic. Where induction relies on multiple experiences to support a generalization about those experiences, deduction uses a pattern of statements to defend a conclusion. Perhaps the best-known early example is the following:

All humans are mortal. (major proposition)

Socrates is a human. (minor proposition)

Therefore, Socrates is mortal. (conclusion)

Each statement here is called a **proposition**; the last one is the **conclusion**, and it is supported by the first two, called, in turn, the major proposition and minor proposition. As you can see, the first statement is a generalization and the second is a particular example. Essentially, this three-part form places a general subject in a class, then places a particular subject in a class, then concludes by observing that the particular subject must have the same property as the general because they belong to the same class (mortal humans). We have said, "All a's are b; c is an a; therefore, c is also a b." If we do this in the correct form and if the propositions are true, then the reasoning will be both sound and valid. The point to remember here is that we arrive at the general truth through the **operation of logic** rather than the enumeration of particular instances. If we wished to arrive at this conclusion inductively, we would have to **list many instances** of people we knew who had died before offering the "Socrates is mortal" conclusion.

This is necessarily a simplified description of the syllogism, the main feature of traditional reasoning. You can learn more about syllogistic logic by asking your instructor. What is important to grasp here is the fact that you can establish something about a particular subject by linking it to a general observation; you don't have to keep multiplying your examples.

If we apply deductive reasoning to the earlier subject of global warming, we could say, "Ice that is warmed will shrink; the arctic glaciers are shrinking; therefore, the glaciers have been warmed." This is, in fact, one of the means employed by the scientific community to back its point about global warming.

THE TOULMIN MODEL OF ARGUMENT

Stephen Toulmin, a British philosopher, felt that syllogistic logic was too difficult for the average writer to use comfortably in writing an argument. In his book *The Uses of Argument* (Cambridge, 1958), Toulmin said,

> Ever since Aristotle it has been customary, when analysing the micro-structure of arguments, to set them out in a very simple manner: they have been presented three propositions at a time, "minor premiss; major premiss; *so* conclusion".... Can we properly classify all the elements in our arguments under the three headings, "major premiss", "minor premiss" and "conclusion", or are these categories misleadingly few in number? (96)*

From this starting point, Toulmin went on to suggest we would be better to copy the field of law and its practices in constructing arguments. He ended by explaining three major terms and three minor terms he believed would replace the Aristotelian terms and serve us better in the building of an argument.

Toulmin's three major terms are **data**, **claim**, and **warrant**.

- The **claim** is, of course, the central aim of the argument. However, the mass of the argument is devoted to support of that claim, whether through examples, reasoning, or counterargument.

- The **data** are the source of the reasoned appeal of an argument. We must offer our readers reasons why our **claim** is a valid one, one they can accept. Arguing differs from proclaiming in always stressing the reasons for acceptance in concrete,

---

*Excerpt from *The Uses of Argument*, by Stephen Toulmin (Cambridge: Cambridge University Press, 1958).

fact-based reasoning. Whether we use inductive or deductive means, we have to include data to support our claims. If we want to make the **claim** that coal-based generator stations are going to increase the carbon dioxide in the atmosphere, we need support. Simply saying that the air smells noxious when we are close to such a plant is not a fact but an impression. If, however, we can go to an expert witness and discover that, while coal accounts for only twenty-five percent of the electricity generated globally, it causes thirty-nine percent of "energy-related carbon dioxide emissions,"* we have a **fact-based support** for our claim.

- It is easiest to understand **warrant** by connecting it to another of its forms, "warranting" or even "warranty." We know a warranty guarantees the quality of a product by assuring the customer a replacement if the product breaks before the warranty expires. We understand the warrant issued by a court is a fact-based reason or reasons why a judge should grant the government the right to search a premises or arrest somebody. In Toulmin's model, *warrant* means the logic or reasoning that guarantees the offered facts are a sufficient support of the claim's validity. What the writer has to decide, in each claim-based paragraph, is whether or not the warrant has to be explicitly stated or whether the reader can be trusted to infer the connection from the facts. In the example above, the fourteen percent discrepancy between the generation of electricity and the generation of carbon dioxide is an inferred warrant that the fuel used in this case is dirtier than other fossil fuels when burned. In each paragraph you write in an argument using the Toulmin model, you therefore have to decide whether to trust your reader to infer the connection between claim and data or whether to supply it directly.

The three additional terms Toulmin suggested for use in constructing arguments are **backing**, **rebuttal**, and **qualifier**.

___

*Excerpt from *The Vancouver Sun*, 24 March 2008, D8.

- The term **backing** is attached to the process of warranting. Suppose, in the above case, that we did not feel the simple numerical difference between twenty-five percent and thirty-nine percent was sufficient to make the case for coal's being the dirtiest of the fossil fuels; we would then attach more fact-based support to the warrant. In this case, if we knew that countries with heavy coal-based generation created more carbon dioxide per megawatt of electricity produced than countries generating electricity by other means, we could add that fact to our warrant as an additional guarantee that coal was indeed the culprit.

- **Rebuttal** is really the same element as counterargument or refutation, but it is accomplished in a briefer way. It also can be an **exception** rather than a refutation. In the case we have been using—the "dirtiness" of coal as a fuel—we could establish an exception if all the coal-fired generating stations had the best current scrubbing and filtering elements included to reduce the release of carbon dioxide. That exception would not have much force, however, if the output of carbon dioxide still exceeded alternative forms of generating energy even after the scrubbing and filtering. More often, of course, we attempt to rebut the argument of the position that opposes our position.

- A **qualifier** is, like rebuttal, an element related to the warrant. It relates directly to the force of the warrant. There will be cases when the warrant is absolute and cases where it is not. When we introduce qualifiers like "generally" and "probably," we are qualifying the force of our claim's truth, advising our readers that the truth we are stating is a provisional rather than an absolute truth.

One way of clarifying the structure proposed by Toulmin is to reproduce, in diagrammatic form, the argument we have been referring to about the "dirtiness" of coal-based energy.

Data —————————— **Qualifier**

Burning coal to generate electricity creates 39% of the world's carbon dioxide emissions while producing 25% of the world's electricity

So, probably

Claim
It is a poor choice for use in generating electricity

Since **Warrant** —————— *Unless* **Rebuttal**

We know that carbon dioxide emissions are the chief cause of global warming

The emissions are reduced more than 60% by scrubbers and filtering elements

Because **Backing**
The 2007 announcement from leading environmental scientists was adopted by the UN

This example demonstrates the way the Toulmin model can be used to build an argument. Once you are familiar with the six terms and can hold them comfortably in your head while you write, you should be able to write an academic argument that is fact- and reason-based. Additionally, simply applying the three major terms as an **editing tool** when you revise your essay will ensure you have relevant facts supporting claims (and warrants where necessary) in each of your working paragraphs.

7-c Common Errors in Writing Academic Essays

Years of experience dealing with academic papers at different levels have shown us that there are a relatively limited number of weaknesses that recur in student writing, particularly in the early years of a college/university program. They include

- the use of unsupported claims in paragraphs
- the absence of specific development in paragraphs
- the general absence of definition from the analysis
- the absence of sufficient facts from the writing
- the inability to write effective rebuttals
- a weak or incomplete or poorly focused thesis

THE USE OF UNSUPPORTED CLAIMS IN PARAGRAPHS

Using unsupported claims is a frequent occurrence in first-year papers that stems from a misunderstanding of how the standard academic paragraph works. For some reason, the writer confuses claims and warrants (see the Toulmin model in 7-b) and uses one generalization to support another. For instance, assume that the writer is making the claim in a paragraph that non-traditional hockey markets are a financial drain on the rest of the league. The writer offers, as a defence, the statement that traditional teams have more financial resources. This is, however, simply another claim, and the paragraph now contains two unsupported claims instead of one. At best, this reveals a vague thought process; at worst, it offers assertions that are undefended and therefore of little worth.

The writer of such a paragraph simply hasn't learned that a paragraph in academic writing can usually accommodate only one claim; the rest of the paragraph is devoted to supporting that claim and linking it to the overall analysis. This fact is not limited to those assignments described as "arguments." The necessity for specific supports and warranting for a claim exists in all academic writing.

Whatever the reason, nothing leads more certainly to failure in a paper than the inability to offer specific factual supports for general claims. When you are editing your paper, use one dedicated sweep to check how you supported your claims. Did you include facts? Did you connect the fact or facts to your claim through warranting where necessary? Did you ever support a claim with another claim? You may even want to use differently coloured highlighting, whether manual or electronic, to identify claims and supports as you go through your essay.

THE ABSENCE OF SPECIFIC DEVELOPMENT IN PARAGRAPHS

The lack of specific development is closely related to the lack of support for a claim and often reveals itself by the presence of many short paragraphs in a paper. While it is simplistic to suggest there should be some standard length for paragraphs in academic writing, it is fair to point out that three- and four-sentence paragraphs are likely to be successful only when they are used as transition paragraphs.

The general work of a paragraph in an academic paper is to establish a claim and to link that claim to the other claims in the analysis or argument. Usually, that will take five to ten sentences to accomplish. You need specific supports, a sentence or two warranting the connection between the supports and the general claim, and perhaps some definitional work. You can't do that in three or four sentences.

THE GENERAL ABSENCE OF DEFINITION FROM THE ANALYSIS

In academic writing, the exact meaning of a term is important, particularly if the success of the analysis depends on your reader having the same meaning in mind as you do. This is an important enough matter to require you to engage in more than denotative definition. It is a simple act to cite a definition provided by a dictionary, but it may not serve your purpose sufficiently. You may need to provide a stipulative definition, one where you specify your intended meaning and link it to your larger purposes. Stipulative definitions use the history of a word, contrast, usage, and many other means to arrive at a complex and complete definition to be shared with the reader. Any time you are dealing with a subject where a term has significant and diverse meanings, offer a definition.

THE ABSENCE OF SUFFICIENT FACTS

The lack of sufficient facts is always a revealing deficiency. Generally, a paragraph needs only one claim but multiple facts. The absence of facts or concrete support tells you most typically that you are not ready to write the analysis you had in mind. You need to gather more facts and concrete support before continuing. A quick way of checking the proportions of fact and generalization in your essay is to use highlighting to isolate claims and supports for claims. That should tell you quickly if your proportions are reasonable.

THE INABILITY TO WRITE EFFECTIVE REBUTTALS

The rebuttal or refutation or counterargument is a common feature in academic writing. Rebuttal is essential in an argument and helps the credibility of your position by honestly responding to opposing positions. It is also frequently present in analytical essays when the analysis attempts to be persuasive.

You can construct a rebuttal very simply. First, write a neutral and complete account of the opposing argument. Second, deal with any concessions you want to make to that position; remember that you don't have to dismiss it entirely. Third, identify the one or two or three most vulnerable premises in that position. With the aid of facts, state why you have problems accepting that position.

A WEAK OR INCOMPLETE OR POORLY FOCUSED THESIS

Many times, the real problem in an academic essay is the overall position that is supposed to drive it. The term *thesis* describes the overall position or purpose of a paper. Whether you prefer to use a term like "controlling claim" or some other term, you will agree that a weakness in this part of an essay will be quite damaging.

To understand the thesis more exactly, remember that it has two parts, not one. A thesis names a subject or issue and asserts a perspective on that subject/issue. Sometimes, the weakness in the thesis is simply the fact that the subject is named but no clear position is defined on that subject. A successful thesis is never general or fuzzy. Consider the following theses:

> A non-traditional team, because of its weaker financial base, cannot compete successfully with a traditional team.

> Although there are occasional exceptions, non-traditional teams in today's professional sports leagues cannot compete equally in the long term with teams whose markets and revenue bases are historically, more entrenched in the community.

What should be apparent to you is that the more successful theses are those that include necessary concessions, avoid universal or categorical positions, and offer reasonably exact terms. Before you become deeply immersed in drafting your paper, check to see if your thesis has sufficient depth and clarity to sustain your analysis or argument.

SUMMARY 8

A summary is a condensed version of the text expressed in your own words (see Chapter 16). Ideally, your summary should occupy about thirty percent of the space taken up by the original. You would typically create a file for each major resource consulted and store your summaries there, along with paraphrases and direct quotations. Remember that you are usually interested in the claims or lead ideas and not in the supports offered for those ideas or claims.

The following guidelines will help you develop a summary:

1. Read the passage. As you read, concentrate on gaining a comprehensive understanding of the author's intention. If the passage is in a book you own, you might want to highlight or underline key points as you read.

2. Re-read the passage.

3. Find the major claim in the first paragraph of the passage; write down the claim on a separate piece of paper. Do the same for the second and subsequent paragraphs.

4. Eliminate all illustrations or examples that may appear in these paragraphs, unless an illustration is an integral part of the claim.

5. Examine any definitions that appear in the paragraphs of the passage; decide if they are important enough to retain.

6. If you copy a phrase of the original passage, make sure you identify it as a quotation so that you will know to treat it as such if you subsequently use the phrase in your own work. Remember, too, that if you summarize a passage and use it in your work, you will need to give a reference for the material, so make sure that you copy down the page number for a citation.

7. Once you have assembled the raw materials for your summary (claims, essential definitions, illustrations, dates, facts), use them to help you write the first draft.

8. As you write your first draft, remember to express the main points of the passage in your own words.

9. Check your first draft to see that it includes all the essential material and is written in your own words. Edit the draft for unnecessary repetition and wordy expression, and look for places where you can combine or condense statements.

10. Write a final draft in which you concentrate on clarity and effective sequencing.

9 WRITING A LITERARY ANALYSIS

A literary analysis requires you to present and defend an argument based on your interpretation of a text. Depending on the topic, a literary analysis will contain some or all of the elements associated with each of its three major parts: the introduction, the body paragraphs, and the concluding paragraph. For more information about special types of paragraphs, see Chapter 35.

9-a Introduction

The opening paragraph (or paragraphs) of a literary analysis must name the topic, state the writer's position on that topic, and provide any background necessary to an understanding of that position. The introduction may also preview the argument to be presented and define any terms critical to the argument. The introduction of a literary analysis will include most of the following elements:

1. *General opening comment.* This comment names your topic and, if necessary, the context in which it appears.

2. *Focusing statement.* The focusing statement narrows the subject area named in your opening sentence and expresses your position on the topic.

3. *Explanatory statement(s).* This element provides any information that is necessary to clarify the opening comment or focusing statement. For example, an explanatory statement might provide a definition of a key term used in the opening comment or clarify the context in which the topic is being analyzed. Often more than one sentence is needed to communicate this information.

4. *Thesis statement.* The thesis statement expresses in specific terms the central point of your argument. A thesis statement typically appears at the end of the introductory paragraph(s).

5. *Overview of your argument.* Like the preview element in the introductory paragraph of an essay (see Chapter 35), this optional element provides readers with a sense of the direction your argument will take.

To sum up, the introductory elements outlined above involve the following activities:

Naming ➤ Narrowing ➤ Explaining ➤ Stating ➤ Previewing

9-b Body Paragraphs

The argument used to prove a thesis is presented in the body paragraphs of the literary analysis. Remember that the sentences that make up a body paragraph should follow a clear and logical sequence, and that each paragraph should advance your overall argument.

The following model is one of many you could use to construct a body paragraph:

1. Use your first sentence as a *transition*, a bridge that connects one paragraph to the next.

2. The second sentence, called a *claim sentence*, is one in which you present the next claim you make in your argument.

3. The claim sentence is followed by the *definitional or background sentence*, in which you present all the background information necessary to your claim. You may require more than one sentence to accomplish this task.

4. The fourth task, called a *demonstrating position*, requires you to prove your claim. In this part of the paragraph, you write as many sentences as are needed to present the logic and evidence that supports your claim. Support may take the form of a simple illustration or example.

5. In this model, you conclude by specifying how the paragraph's claim relates to and advances the overall argument.

To sum up, the body-paragraph model outlined above involves the following activities:

Connecting ➤ Claiming ➤ Defining or Restricting ➤ Proving ➤ Relating

9-c Concluding Paragraph

The concluding paragraph of a literary analysis typically contains the following elements:

1. *Summary*. The summary encapsulates the main points of the argument. Unless your argument is unusually complex, your summary should generally not run longer than three sentences.

2. *Restatement*. The restatement is a concise and emphatic reiteration of your thesis.

3. *Indication of general significance*. This optional element provides some indication of the general

significance of your thesis by pointing out its connection to a larger topic. For example, you might relate your thesis to a recurrent pattern in the writer's work or some general observation about human behaviour.

Whether it ends with a restatement or with an indication of general significance, your concluding paragraph should convey an impression of finality; readers should be left with the sense that nothing of importance remains to be said.

To sum up, the concluding-paragraph elements outlined above involve the following activities:

Summarizing ➤ Restating ➤ Signifying

WRITING IN THE SOCIAL SCIENCES 10

AN OVERVIEW

The social sciences turn a scientific eye upon some facet or dimension of society. They assume that all or part of the scientific method can be employed to improve our ability to understand who individual humans or social units are and what dynamics make them distinctive. The scientific method is normally used to identify the complex of perspectives and practices that arrived in the seventeenth and eighteenth centuries to enable the human intellect to study problems and then both propose and test possible answers to these problems through close observation. Where the sciences observe the physical world, the social sciences observe the human world. The intent of each, however, is to replace intuition and unaided viewing with logic, experiment, and the creation and proving of hypotheses.

The first principle for a student entering a social science discipline to grasp, therefore, is the need for proof, for staking a claim on something more reliable than insight, patterning, or textual analysis. Any thesis or general claim that you base a paper on will have to be proven empirically or logically. The conundrum for the social scientists, whether they are looking at groups or at individuals, is that humans are not easily captured through logic alone and not always susceptible to empirical testing. Nevertheless, get ready to emphasize claims based on shared and explored data, the central mode of analytic inquiry in these disciplines.

The range of these subjects can be seen in the following list of topics. Think about what you would need to do to respond successfully to them.

- Review three influential theories of dreaming. In your review, suggest strengths and deficits in each.

- Choose one significant immigrant group in your province that has been present for at least two generations and identify the forces that have pushed them toward segregation or integration. Provide an estimate of how far the third generation has moved toward segregation or integration with the majority culture.

- Examine the social behaviour patterns exhibited by the society in the film *Brave*.

- In Canada, over a period of twenty years—from 1985 to 2005—production of goods has increased by 29% while personal income has increased, in constant terms, by 3.5%. Account for these quite different rates.

Each of these topics would require a significant response and generate a paper of six to fifteen pages. Each would mean you would have to research, adopt a thesis or general claim to provide a centre for your inquiry, and employ empirical and/or abstract proving to get your audience to accept your claim. Think about how you might do that and what kinds of proving you would employ.

WHAT VOICE SHOULD I USE?

In humanities subjects, students are often urged to include personal experience and response to phenomena. In most humanities subjects, the professor or instructor is not concerned if you use personal pronouns in your writing. The social sciences prefer that you cultivate an impersonal voice and write without personal pronouns. In a humanities essay, you might say "I noted Walter Abrahams' insistence that immigrant groups will necessarily move toward integration over the course of a few generations unless they can retain physical and cultural distinctiveness." In a social sciences essay, you are more likely to use the following voice: "Immigrant groups lose their sense of distinctiveness and begin to blend with the majority culture over time unless they can preserve separateness through cultural and linguistic distinctiveness (Abrahams, 1998, p. 46)." You should check with your instructor as to what voice—personal or impersonal—he or she prefers in an essay.

HOW SHOULD I REASON IN THIS SUBJECT?

The ideal in the social sciences is to support a claim or hypothesis with evidence and reasoning. As with any academic essay, the major claim is given early, often in the first paragraph, and the body paragraphs contain the sub-claims, empirical data, and reasoning that, together, persuade the reader of the validity of that general claim. You will also be called on, in some essay assignments, to apply principles and theories from that discipline to a problem. It is important, therefore, to learn something about the fundamental modes of reasoning.

One way to begin is to refresh your understanding of two basic methods of establishing a claim. The method we learn most frequently in our early years is called **induction**, the assembling of multiple examples to establish a general claim. Induction can be as simple as touching hot surfaces several times and learning that they hurt. It also can be as complex as assembling statistics to prove what the television-viewing preferences are in Canada. In each case, multiple concrete instances form the sample from which you construct the general claim.

The major elements in a successful induction are the number and kind of examples you use. Statistical sampling recognizes the importance of the population or sample you are surveying. When you read in a newspaper a poll intended to predict the outcome of an election, the polling firm will normally state how many people were interviewed to complete the poll. As well as ensuring that a sample is large enough to support a claim reliably, you also have to ensure the sample is representative. If the pollsters, for instance, have questioned people only in Calgary and Montreal about a national election, they should not predict how Canadians are going to vote. Ideally, therefore, a successful induction employs a sample that is **known**, **sufficient in size**, and **representative** rather than narrow. Social sciences, such as psychology and sociology, rely frequently on induction as the reasoned support for their claims, whether the induction takes the form of a questionnaire, statistics drawn from census results, or a controlled observation of human subjects. You need to gain experience in using this mode of reasoning as supports for the claims you will make in a social sciences paper.

The second form of reasoning works in a reverse direction. **Deduction** starts with a general truth and applies that truth to a particular circumstance to create a new conclusion or prediction. In its oldest form, deduction uses a syllogism, a three-part statement terminating in a conclusion. The following is a simple illustration of this form:

> All individual humans are people who have rights.
> Children are individual humans.
> Therefore, children are people who have rights.

You are unlikely to employ deduction in this restrictive format, but it allows you to see the purpose and form of this kind of reasoning, moving to a particular conclusion by applying a general truth to a specific subject.

Consider the earlier subject about the gap between the growth of productivity and the growth of income. You might start to unlock the subject by applying a general truth, such as the phenomenon in industrial and post-industrial societies that income generated by the economy is not evenly distributed throughout the population. Applying that to the general data presented in the topic could lead you to the beginnings of a controlling claim for your analysis. The point here is that, instead of using multiple concrete examples as a foundation for a generalization, you are applying a general truth to a particular circumstance or circumstances.

FOCUSED RESEARCH

One way to approach an assignment is to read everything you can find on a subject. A second way is to form a hypothesis or provisional position on your subject and then conduct a more focused search.

Again using the previous example, you might decide that the only explanation for the discrepancy between production growth and income stagnation was that the income produced by selling the greater amount of goods was chiefly going into the pockets of a few, or that it was taxed away. This would give you a sharper focus and you could create a preliminary reading list and start to make your notes.

ARGUMENT AND ANALYSIS: THE FINISHED PAPER

Are you writing to inform?

If so, description and comprehensive presentation are your allies, along with a full supply of facts and data.

Are you writing to critique?

If so, you need a survey of what has been said about your subject by others and either a synthesis of those views or a critical review of them and a presentation of your own position. If a critical review is required, you have to summarize the view fairly as a first step, then move to your areas of agreement and disagreement with that view. In doing so, you want to pay special attention to features like unexamined assumptions in the view, breadth and applicability of the view, currency of sampling or examples (if they are a major support), and discrepancies between this view and other views you are surveying.

Are you writing to argue?

If so, you need to have a sense of how to structure and conduct an argument. One valuable aid for this is the Toulmin form of argument (see 7-b). It offers a model that can ensure you present a comprehensive and reasoned position. The three primary terms—claim, data, and warrant —will give your argument a structure and will also ensure each part of that argument is based on reasoning. The three secondary terms—rebuttal, qualifier, and backing—will strengthen your reasoning and ensure that it is both balanced and fair.

A **claim** and **data** are terms that are self-explanatory. Remember also that you have both a **controlling claim** as a centre in your paper and **supporting claims** that form the development and proof for your thesis (controlling claim).

Rebuttal allows you to canvass an opposing view and concede anything you wish to that view while still advancing your own position. **Qualifiers** are necessary any time you are not making an absolute claim, which is most of the time. And **backing** adds depth to your argument, an important quality.

The heart of any arguing, however, lies in the making of claims supported by fact, expert witness, or logic. Many writers don't realize that the key movement in a supporting paragraph is the explanation of why the offered support can prove that the claim is credible. Using the structure offered by Toulmin is consistent with the tests for probability demanded by the social sciences and its parts force you to complete your logic.

AN EXAMPLE

Consider the topic on the gap between production gains and income stasis as an example where you can gain credibility by applying the Toulmin terms as a reference and skeletal structure for your argument.

You have already chosen a provisional hypothesis—that the gap between what happened with production and income is best explained by the fact that production profits are unequally shared by the population. In your research, you will need to gather data to support that hypothesis, create warranting to link the data logically to your central claim/hypothesis, and rebut any opposing explanations. You can find data on the unequal distribution of profits in Statistics Canada publications or in provincial government statistics. In fact, any introductory economics text will provide such data.

You have to develop your central claim more fully, establish in 1985 dollars that incomes have remained static, and suggest why this might have happened. Otherwise, all you have is an unsupported claim.

Let's say you have checked the gain, year over year, of revenues from private income tax in the first decade of the twenty-first century. At the same time, you have data showing the increase in productivity within the economy for the same period as the gain in new jobs. You want to make a supporting claim for your central position that the gap is principally a result of unequal distribution of profits. The data tell you that the percentage gain in new jobs in the period is greater than the percentage gain in revenue from taxation of private incomes.

Here is where **warranting** comes to your rescue. Without it, you have a claim and data but no proof. Just like the petitioner for a warrant in the justice system, you want your audience, and especially your instructor, to believe you have supported your claim with valid reasoning.

To return to the general claim about the gap between income and productivity growth, you have to use **inference**, the act of offering a link between two facts, to show that the new jobs provided a less than average income. That's why the tax revenue didn't increase comparably. You then show, statistically, that the greater production created considerable new income and thus prove that the money was not distributed equally. Here, then, is one completed and warranted proof for your hypothesis.

Another view, however, holds that this gap can be explained by a change in tax policy, a reduction in base income tax. To deal with that position, you have to move to **rebuttal**, one of the three secondary Toulmin terms. Assume, for the purpose of the example, that you have data showing that 75% of the tax adjustments benefited the top 10% of the population. You can then demonstrate that the remaining 25%, spread among 90% of the population, cannot sufficiently explain the gap. In rebutting, you state the other side's position fairly, show what that position rests on in terms of proof, and introduce a data-based claim to reveal that position is partially or completely wrong. In this case, you have illustrated that it is partially wrong. This will lead you to use a **qualifier**, such as the word "sufficiently." The other position cannot show why the majority of the gap exists, and therefore its proof is insufficient.

In the social sciences, you want to take a position and then use inductive or deductive proofs on which it can rest. This mingling of claiming, concrete facts and inferences, and warranting is quite basic to academic writing and particularly important for attaining the probability that the social sciences wish to have for their analyses and arguments.

APA style: some guidelines

Here are a few additional points that might assist you in writing your paper in a social sciences field.

Two introduction models

The introduction of your essay is always a critical part. You want that first paragraph to background your topic and profile your main claim. Occasionally, you will write an inquiry paper where the central claim or thesis emerges slowly rather than being presented at he very beginning. However, that is infrequently the case.

One kind of opening paragraph backgrounds the topic or subject, narrows the focus, offers any key definitions, and conveys the central claim.

A second kind of introduction relies on a more standardized opening. The early sentences identify the subject, background it so that the reader will see what facet of it is the true subject, possibly review/present two divergent views of the issue/subject, and then conclude "This essay will . . ." so that your intention is explicitly signalled.

Ask your instructor if he or she prefers the latter opening to the former.

Presenting statistics

You will frequently have to insert data into your essay and should know some basic principles for doing so. Visual aids either orient a reader (maps, cross-sections, charts) or present data visually (tables, graphs) to make it more easily understood. You should be able to identify these aids and know how and when to include them to make your paper stronger.

The *Publications Manual of the American Psychological Association*, sixth edition, divides all the visual figures you might use into two groupings: **tables** and **figures**.

A **table** is the correct term for data presented in ranks or columns. It is organized this way so that the reader can absorb large amounts of information in an accessible format. Normally, a table divides its data into columns and rows; for instance, the columns could represent Years, and the rows could represent Failure Rates in Grade 12 Mathematics Provincial Finals for each of those years. Place the identifying title *above the table* and flush with the left margin. If you have only two or three tables in your paper, identify them serially as Table 1, Table 2, and Table 3. However, when you have several tables focused on a single aspect of your subject, identify your tables as Table 1.1, Table 1.2, and so on.

For assistance in creating and critiquing tables in your paper (or someone else's), consult the Table Checklist on page 150 of the *APA Manual*, sixth edition.

Figures include **graphs**, **charts**, **maps**, **drawings**, **diagrams**, and **photographs**. When information is transformed into a visual mode so that relationships can be graphically captured and presented in a snapshot or over time, a **figure** is the appropriate choice. Place the title of the figure flush left *below the figure*. If you have a limited number of these, simply call them Figure 1, Figure 2, and

Figure 3. If, however, a number of them are clustered around one of your subjects, identify them as Figure 1.1, Figure 1.2, and Figure 1.3. Of the various kinds of figures available to you, one of them needs further explanation: the graph.

A **graph** is a visual presentation of data. The best known are **bar graphs** with a vertical or horizontal scale and bars representing the relationship among different measures. This kind of graph is excellent for contrasting differences in the elements being measured and compared. A **line graph** presents measures changing over time and shows them plotted on lines so the viewer can see how the relationships between or among what is measured varies. A **pie graph**, sometimes called a pie chart, divides a circle into "slices" of "pie" of varying widths to show their relative relationships. It's a good choice any time you want to divide a whole into parts to show how they relate, as you might if you want to show the relative expenditures in a provincial budget on highways, family service, education, and health.

For assistance in assessing and creating figures, consult the Figure Checklist on p. 167 of the APA *Manual*, sixth edition.

Occasionally, you have to convey scientific phenomena or a wiring pattern or something visually complicated. You need to use a **diagram** for this kind of data. However, it should still be identified as a figure.

Using headings

Some disciplines approve the use of headings within your essay to distinguish one part of that essay or report from another. The sixth edition of the *APA Publication Manual* describes how to create headings in an appropriately predictable way. Pages 62 and 63 of the *Manual* give you the five levels of headings used in APA journals. If you are ever in need of multiple levels of headings for an assignment, this entry provides a functional guide.

EXAM STRATEGIES 11

To write an effective essay exam, you must be able to apply general skills, such as *recall, interpretation, time management,* and *focused writing.* An essay exam also requires you to apply critical thinking skills, such as *inference, causal analysis, summary, analysis, evaluation,* and *synthesis.*

Do not wait until the last moment to prepare for an exam. You should study throughout the term, and you should carry out your studies in a systematic fashion. Establish and follow a realistic schedule of study activities, such as summarizing key content, mastering new terms and concepts, and working on difficult topics. Let your understanding of the material dictate how much time you devote to studying. You might consider using a six-step weekly study schedule:

1. Read new material.

2. Take notes.

3. Relate new material to material you have already learned.

4. Review material from the preceding week.

5. Make a note of material you think you should review again the following week.

6. Review material you have not mastered in previous weeks.

As a complement to independent study, you can establish a study group that meets on a regular basis. Reviewing and discussing course material with your peers is a good way to test your grasp of that material.

Use the following lists of strategies as a general guide for all your exam preparations.

11-a Before the Exam

Review your study materials.

- Review your summary notes from the course.
- Combine your lecture and summary notes.
- Highlight or underline in your notes key ideas, key concepts, and terms for special study.
- Create a glossary (including definitions) of key terms introduced in the course.
- Select evidence to support each key idea.
- Note the connections among key ideas.
- Use your organized list of key ideas as a study guide.

11-b During the Exam

1. *Use the first five to ten minutes of the allotted exam time to read, plan, and organize.*

- Read the instructions before you do anything else.

- Quickly write down any important facts, definitions, or formulas you think you will need and are afraid you will forget.

- Decide whether the questions ask for definitions, problem solving, application of knowledge, or explanations. Underline the key words and verbs employed in the questions. Remember that different verbs, such as *analyze* and *compare,* require you to do different things. See 12-d for definitions of verbs you will encounter in both exam questions and research essay instructions.

- Develop a strategy for handling the exam in general and each question in particular. If the exam gives you choices, make your choices now. Decide where to start.

- Divide the exam time according to the marks awarded for each question, factoring in the time you allotted to planning and editing.

- Stick to the time you allot yourself for each answer. If you think one answer needs more time, you can always leave some blank space at the end of your answer and come back to that answer when you finish the rest of the exam.

- List relevant points for the question you want to answer first and arrange the points in an effective sequence.

- Use the points to develop a thesis or claim (or rephrase the question to formulate a thesis). Remember that your thesis must address the question you are asked. Some students like to incorporate the actual words of the question into their opening statement.

- Stick to the topic and use specific evidence to support your points.

- Remember that each paragraph should relate to your thesis and to the previous paragraph.

- Your conclusion should provide a restatement of the thesis, a summary of the main points, and a comment that synthesizes your argument.

2. *While writing, budget your time and try to write complete, well-organized answers.*

   - Use only one side of the exam-book pages. Double-space essay and paragraph answers so that you leave yourself room to make additions and corrections when you read over your work. Use the other side of the exam-book pages for your rough work or corrections.

   - Use vocabulary that is appropriate to the exam's discipline.

   - Make use of theories or arguments that are relevant to the topic.

   - Analyze: don't list or summarize unless the question asks you to do so.

   - Make relevant connections between points and explain information clearly.

   - Watch the time. If you find you have too much information and not enough time, you will have to edit your argument or use point form.

3. *Use the closing minutes of exam time to revise, edit, and proofread.*

   - People who mark exams are primarily interested in the organization and content of your answers. Remember that a proofreading sweep (which eliminates errors in spelling, usage, and punctuation) is not as important as the content, coherence, and logic of your answer.

   - Ask yourself these simple editing questions:
     - Have I supported each of my points?
     - Are my facts correct, clearly stated, and relevant?
     - Does each paragraph support and extend my argument? (If a paragraph is irrelevant, delete it.)

11-c Multiple-Choice and Short-Answer Exams

- Some examiners who use multiple-choice exams subtract the number of wrong answers from the number of right answers. If the exam instructions indicate that this is the case, be cautious about guessing.

- In a long exam with a large number of multiple-choice or short-answer questions, start at the beginning and work through the questions in the order in which they appear.

- On your first pass through an exam, respond only to questions whose answers you are sure of. Later, return to questions you have not answered.

- Be careful with multiple-choice questions that have two or more similar answers. If you are not sure of the answer, come back to the question later.

- Remember that short answers should be unified and to the point.

- Always leave enough time to review and revise your answers.

Research
Essays

Whenever you write a research essay or report, you engage in the research process. The seven-step system described in this section is designed to smooth your progress through this complex process.

STEP 1: DEFINING THE ASSIGNMENT

12

Your first task in any research essay is to conduct an analysis of the research assignment. A fundamental part of that analysis is defining your audience, purpose, and scope; clarifying the assignment instructions; and determining your research requirements.

12-a Audience

The voice you adopt in your essay, the vocabulary you use, and the stance you take will depend on your understanding of your audience and its expectations. Ask yourself the following questions:

- If the audience is specified in the assignment, what are the expectations of that audience? How well informed is the audience about the assignment topic?
- If the audience is not specified, should I seek guidance from my instructor or should I address a generalized audience?
- If the audience is my instructor, what are his or her expectations?
- Is the audience likely to have a position on the topic? What is it?
- What response do I want to elicit from my audience?

12-b Purpose

Purpose refers to the aim or objective of your essay. Does the topic provide opportunities for you to *describe, inform, recommend, evaluate, argue, interpret,* or some combination of these?

Before you complete the preliminary phase of your research project, you should know the answers to these questions:

- What is the purpose of the assignment? Is the purpose explicitly stated or is it implied?

- Am I being asked to write a demonstration essay? Am I to show I have mastered certain concepts in the specified field?

- Am I invited to define my own approach or is an approach assigned to me?

- If an argument is called for, are the terms of the argument given in the assignment?

12-c Scope

Scope refers to the breadth or range of the assignment. To define the scope of an essay, ask yourself these questions:

- Does the assignment specify the extent or range of the research that will be required?

- Does the assignment specify the length of the essay?

- Are the terms supplied in the assignment general or specific?

- If the terms are general, does the assignment give me the option of defining them more precisely?

- Is the assignment "open" in the sense that it allows me to create my own topic or scope?

12-d The Instructions

One of the first things you should do when you get a research assignment is analyze the instructions. Consider the following sample assignments:

- *Analyze* the major choices in presentation software available to a mid-sized firm and *recommend* the package your firm should purchase.

- *Evaluate* the major features that caused large audiences to return faithfully to the episodes of the various *Survivor* series.

The verbs indicate the tasks you are being asked to perform as a writer. You should underline such verbs in the assignment instructions and, using the following glossary as a guide, specify the demands each verb makes.

- *Account for* asks you to perform causal analysis— that is, use supporting detail to demonstrate how and why a particular phenomenon occurred.

- *Analyze* means to take something apart to see how it works. In an analysis, you may examine the parts, steps, sections, or causes of your topic (compare with *synthesize*).

- *Assess* requires you to examine a topic critically to determine its value or significance.

- *Compare* asks you to examine two or more topics to find and explore similarities.

- *Contrast* requires you to examine two or more topics to find and explore differences.

- *Defend* asks you to express a particular position and defend it.

- *Define* requires you to invent your definition by (1) drawing on your research; (2) using the classical defining mechanism of placing your topic in the class to which it belongs and then distinguishing it from all other members of that class; (3) employing an invented definition; or (4) using such definitional techniques as history and background, comparison and contrast, or context. A definitional essay does not mean defining a few terms; it asks you to make definition the entire focus of your essay.

- *Evaluate* asks you to judge a topic. You cannot evaluate without first creating and announcing the criteria or standards you employ in evaluating your topic. It is up to you to establish and defend the criteria of your evaluation.

- *Review* requires you to present a summary of the topic and examine the summary for the purpose of evaluation.

- *Summarize* asks you to express briefly the main points of the topic.

- *Synthesize* requires you to merge, creatively, multiple perspectives (compare with *analyze*).

- *Trace* asks you to ascertain the sequence of, or account for, the stages in the development of the topic.

12-e Research Requirements

To determine what your research requirements are, you must first decide if you need to use primary sources or if you can complete the assignment using secondary sources alone. Primary sources are an integral part of the topic you are writing about, while secondary sources are interpretations of that topic.

STEP 2: DEVELOPING A PRELIMINARY THESIS 13

You can narrow and focus a topic by developing a *preliminary thesis* (also called a *working thesis*). A preliminary thesis has two functions: (1) it names the topic, and (2) it indicates your anticipated position on that topic. One of the easiest ways to arrive at a preliminary thesis is to use the looping technique (see 2-c). The statement you write about can be as simple as *When I think of X, I feel* .... Here are three other techniques you can use to narrow and focus a topic:

1. *Limit the time frame.* If the topic encompasses a twenty-year period, change the time frame to a ten-year period unless your instructor objects.

2. *Limit the geographical scope.* Instead of assessing the impact of the most recent recession on Canada as a whole, concentrate on one region.

3. *Reduce the number of topic elements.* If your topic has three parts, eliminating one of those parts will make it more manageable. If the topic calls for you to compare and contrast four subjects, see what happens when you reduce the number of subjects to two or three.

Once you are satisfied with your preliminary thesis, you can start creating a working bibliography, a list of sources you want to consult or research you want to initiate. If you want to do primary research, you will need specific guidance from your instructor. Secondary research is less challenging, but far more frequently a key part of your preparation when writing a paper for a course. Secondary research involves building a working bibliography of secondary sources. The places where you will most likely initiate this stage are your computer and your institution's library. The person you will most likely consult for assistance in this search is a librarian in your university's library.

14-a Reference Sources: Internet

You can get a quick sense of the sources available to you online by activating a search engine such as Google, Bing, or Yahoo!Search. These days, search engines are integrated into your web browser as an add-on: just type your key terms into the address bar in Google Chrome, Internet Explorer, Firefox, or Apple's Safari. You can also browse the search engine's website and enter your terms there. Although this form of search will get you started, you will soon need to consult a librarian and get advice about the new search tools available to you. Before copying any material, set up a folder for your assignment. Once your assignment folder is established, it becomes a simple task to use the copy and paste commands to move material you want to retain into the appropriate file in that folder.

When you find material online and move it into your file, you must, as a heading in that file, copy the title of the source, the author if one is identified, the name of the website, the URL, and the date you accessed it. If there is a DOI in the source, use the DOI instead of the URL. It is essential to maintain careful records of the sources of your research.

14-b The Google World, Discovery Layers, and Summon

Having begun your research and created a folder for the files you will build as background notes and research, you can move to the next step. As a postsecondary student researching an assigned or chosen topic, you would be inclined to consult Google for assistance. But there are larger and more focused resources available to you.

As you identify the sources you want to use in your research, remember that you will need to check their reliability. For assistance in this evaluation, refer to the advice given in the section on assessing online sources (14-c). Significant changes have occurred in the last decade. The search engines a student researcher might have used in 2003 included names like Microsoft and Time Warner (AOL). Now Google and Bing are clearly dominant, with others providing alternative sources. Because Google is such a vast search engine, it has created a resource specifically for postsecondary researchers called Google Scholar. As a postsecondary student, you will chiefly be using Google Scholar. For a smaller assignment, you might be able to restrict your search to that source. Talk to your librarians about how to use this resource efficiently.

Perhaps the largest difference in recent years is the expansion of search choices for postsecondary students and faculty created by forming library consortia across Canada. Since 2002, the following alliances have been formed:

- Council of Prairie and Pacific University Libraries [COPPUL]: BC, AB, SK, MB

- Ontario Council of University Libraries [OCUL]: ON

- Conference des recteurs et des principaux des universites du Quebec [CREPUQ]: QU

- Council of Atlantic University Libraries [CAUL/CBUA]: NB, NS, PEI, NF

Whichever region you are in, the outreach afforded by these library alliances will establish far wider boundaries for your Internet search than you would get from Google or other search engines: you can now search the libraries of your entire region. You will also be able to bypass the password protections established by universities to stop external searches of their resources. To do that, however, you will need to work from your institution's library.

In conducting a search, therefore, after a preliminary Google Scholar survey, you need to go to a librarian and ask for help in searching your own library's holdings and the resources of your regional alliance.

At this point, you will be introduced to two new terms: *discovery layers* and *Summon*. A simple explanation of these resources would start with discovery layers.

Essentially, discovery layers are the combination of holdings at your postsecondary institution and at the participating institutions in your regional library alliance. You will have a catalogue of all these references, as will the other postsecondary institutions in your region. These catalogues can be searched through the digital interface of the discovery layers. So, whether that resource be a book, a periodical, a magazine, a licensed database, or any other material that is part of any library's resources (as long as it is a member of the regional alliance), it is accessible through a discovery layer search. Again, you will need assistance to conduct your early searches.

A librarian will introduce you to the other key term, Summon. Discovery layers are the aggregated databases represented by your library and the other libraries in the regional alliance. However, you need a way of efficiently searching that enormous storehouse of references.

Summon is the engine that conducts the search you have ordered by typing in subjects and key words. Essentially, discovery layers form an interface comprised of all the holdings in your regional alliance, and Summon is the searcher. The librarian will introduce you to this tool and help you to use it successfully to create your preliminary bibliography. As soon as you enter Summon, you will discover how essential an aid it is for any research assignment. The returns garnered for you by what librarians call Summon Service will, in fact, require you to refine your search. This requirement is discussed further at the end of this section.

Another source on the Internet that searchers utilize is *Wikipedia*, the online encyclopaedia that constantly creates analyses of current subjects and developments. There are critics of *Wikipedia* because it is not a peer-reviewed source and anyone can add to the articles posted there. This is true. However, there is also a committee that reviews each *Wikipedia* entry before it is added. Of more use to you, perhaps, is the fact that *Wikipedia* articles include extensive bibliographies. These bibliographies offer a source you can check against your preliminary bibliography. They have the further attraction of being current bibliographies. Any formally constructed bibliography of readings in a book in your chosen area will be two years old or older because of the publishing process it has been through. But *Wikipedia* adds articles continuously on current as well as older subjects.

Metacrawlers and *metasearch engines* may also assist your search because they survey multiple sites and give you the results of that survey. Metacrawlers are designed to send search requests to various search engines and produce a mix of what they get back in a single offering. This allows you to conduct multiple searches with a single request. Among the leading metacrawlers for accessing the Internet are

Dogpile	http://dogpile.com
Vivisimo	http://vivisimo.com/
Mamma	http:mamma.com

For a fuller account of these resources, you might want to see Chris Sherman's article "Metacrawlers and Metasearch Engines" at http://searchenginewatch.com/article/2066974/metacrawlers-and-metasearch-engines. Meta searching is also possible within the scholarly databases such as those created by EBSCO.

Creating a working bibliography has therefore become both an easier and a more complex task than it was six or seven years ago. For a smaller article/essay, you may find it sufficient to use Google Scholar as your principal search tool. When you are faced with writing a more extensive assignment, you will want to consult with your institution's librarians and get help in employing the extensive search range of discovery layers and Summon.

One key element you will also need assistance with is refining your search. Given that you are able to search comprehensive resources, you will end up with too large a bibliography if you do not manage that search carefully. Consider the following example:

> With the assistance of a Kwantlen librarian, we did a preliminary search for material on hydraulic fracturing, often called "fracking." We searched through EBSCO and through the Summon tool. Our initial response in both cases was massive, 5,000 references through EBSCO and 5,287 through Summon. We then limited the search by refining the title employed in that search, by asking for full-text academic articles only, and by limiting the time line of references to articles published after 2010. These limitations brought the number of references down to 320 from Summon and 186 from EBSCO, a more manageable and relevant number. You could use additional restrictions to get to a number you are

comfortable with. Again, a librarian is an essential guide in your preliminary searching.

The end result should be a list of no more than twenty sources for a large assignment. Remember that, in the formal bibliography that ends your assignment, the safest practice is to restrict your bibliography to those references you've actually used—that is, those you've cited or referred to—in your essay.

14-c Research and the Internet

It takes considerable time and practice to become efficient at using the Internet as a research tool, but your task is greatly simplified if you use a search engine that supports Boolean terms. Boolean terms are words that help define a search. The three primary Boolean terms—AND, OR, and NOT—link topics in order to narrow or expand a search. The Boolean logic associated with each of these terms is described below.

- AND narrows a search by finding only documents containing all of the specified words or phrases. For example, if you search for *cats AND dogs,* only documents containing both words will be retrieved.

- OR expands a search by finding documents containing at least one of the specified words or phrases. For example, if you search for *cats OR dogs,* documents in which either word appears will be retrieved.

- NOT narrows a search by excluding documents containing specified words or phrases. For example, if you search for *cats AND NOT dogs,* all documents containing the word *cats* will be retrieved, except for those documents also containing the word *dogs.* (Note that most search engines will reject your search request if you use the Boolean term NOT alone; preface this term with AND.)

- With some search engines, you can create groupings of terms by putting quotation marks around two or more series of words. When you do this, the search engine will look for each set of words you have set off in quotation marks: for example, "Newfoundland fisheries" AND "seasonal employment in Newfoundland."

STORING AND RETRIEVING INFORMATION

USING COPY AND PASTE TO COLLECT RESEARCH MATERIAL FOR ASSIGNMENTS

When you are working with an online source that allows you to capture material electronically, you will be able to open individual files for each relevant article, write a short header for the file, and save the article in that file. If you later want to utilize this material, you can open a new file, give it a title, and then, using the copy and paste commands of your computer, move important passages from your article file to your new summary file. When you copy and paste material, include the source of the material, the title of the article, the author's name, the relevant page number or numbers (if the pages are numbered), the date of access, and the URL; if a DOI is supplied, use it instead of the URL, and disregard the date of access.

PRINT A HARD COPY OF ARTICLES THAT MAY BE OF USE

You can print a hard copy of the articles you believe will be particularly useful or, better still, save the article to file. This will enable you to use the copy and paste of your word processing program to extract quotations from the article. Since it is hard to digest complex articles fully on a first reading, saving material to a file or printing a copy of it are good research behaviours. If you are printing an article from a service provider, enter your date of access on the first page of the article. As well, be sure your hard copy includes all the information you will need to reference borrowings and to write a bibliographic entry.

TIPS FOR USING ONLINE MATERIAL

- Cut and paste quotations directly into the text of your essay. In doing this, be careful not to introduce typographical or spelling errors, or font inconsistencies, into the body of your essay.

- Set off all direct quotations properly and make sure you attribute your sources for paraphrased or summarized passages with a parenthetical reference (or note) and a bibliographic entry at the end of your essay, depending on the documentation style required by your discipline (see chapters 19–22).

PLAGIARISM AND ONLINE MATERIAL: A WARNING

You must treat any material you gather online in the same manner you would treat material gathered from a book or a journal. More and more plagiarism cases involve students who think that, because they obtained their secondary sources online or electronically, it is not necessary to cite these sources.

ASSESSING ONLINE RESOURCES

The Internet has given us an amazing resource, one that offers access to knowledge from diverse sources. The problem for a person writing a research essay, however, is to distinguish valid information from invalid information. As such, after ordering a search on the Internet about a particular subject and finding fifty or sixty or a hundred suggestions, how should you proceed? The best resource for advice on how to separate the good resource from the bad is provided by *The Columbia Guide to Online Style*, pages 3–27 in particular. Study Tables 1.1 (*Columbia Guide*, pp. 6–13) and 1.2 (*Columbia Guide*, p. 16) to assist your assessment of sources. Pay particular attention to part 1.2 (Evaluating Sources) as a guide.

14-d The Working Bibliography

As you conduct your library and Internet searches, you should continue to build a working bibliography consisting of sources that are relevant to your topic and preliminary thesis. You can record sources in an electronic file or on index cards. Each book and periodical article citation in your working bibliography should include the following (applicable) information:

BOOK	ARTICLE
Call number of book	Author(s) of article
Author(s) of book	Title and subtitle
Title and subtitle	Title of Journal, magazine, or newspaper
Edition and where necessary, editor(s) and translator(s)	Date of publication, and page numbers, edition, and section of the paper (for a newspaper)
City of publication	Volume and issue numbers
Publisher's name	If online, DOI, or URL if no DOI is supplied
Year of publication	Date of access

If online, the website name
If online, DOI, or URL if no
DOI is supplied
If an ebook or online book, the
format of the book
Library and citation information as
you would find them in your library:
Call number: PE 1408 F452 2014
Finnbogason, Jack, and Al Valleau.
A Canadian Writer's Pocket Guide.
5th ed. Toronto: Nelson Education, 2014.

Before you leave this stage of the research process, test the adequacy of your working bibliography by answering these questions:

1. Are all the listed sources relevant to my topic?

2. Do the sources cover all facets of my topic?

3. Are my sources current or are they dated? Is my subject one where currency is important?

4. Is my list balanced? If my subject is one in which opposing positions are taken, have I included at least one reference hostile to my position?

5. Is my working bibliography too ambitious? How much time do I have to complete my research essay and what can I reasonably expect to accomplish within that time?

STEP 4: READING 15

Unlike general readers, researchers are concerned with understanding the strengths and weaknesses of their sources. They read in a structured and systematic fashion and engage in the activities of previewing, note-taking, and taking stock.

15-a Previewing

You should begin the reading process by acquiring an overview of the material. If the source is a book, you can ascertain its general content by reading the preface (if there is one) and last chapter or final paragraphs, and by looking at the table of contents and the index. The table of contents in particular will help you ascertain those parts of the book that are most relevant to your topic. For more information about previewing (and the related techniques of skimming and scanning), see 3-a.

15-b Note-Taking

As you read, take careful, detailed notes. Your note-taking should be systematic. (For a discussion of the mechanics of note-taking, see Chapter 16.) The kinds of notes you take during the reading process will, generally, include the following:

- ideas and facts that either support or contradict your preliminary thesis
- your own questions and comments about the material
- specific examples of the author's biases and assumptions
- any concepts or key terms that are relevant to your topic

15-c Taking Stock

At the conclusion of your reading and note-taking, compile a list of the research tasks that remain. Ask yourself:

- Do I understand all the key terms relevant to my topic?
- What questions arising from my reading do I need to answer?
- Has my preliminary thesis changed as a result of my reading?
- Do I have a good understanding of the strengths and weaknesses of my sources?
- Do I have a good understanding of each author's assumptions or biases?
- Do I have all the sources I need to write about my topic, or do I need additional sources in my working bibliography?

Students and researchers typically take notes on paper or in electronic files. The older system of using note cards has largely given way to computer storage. You still need an efficient storage system and a comprehensive strategy for taking notes. Generally, you should set up a folder for each major written assignment and establish files for each of your significant resources and for your initial draft of your paper.

The first note for each resource should also be your bibliographic note and should record all the data you need for writing a bibliographic note, from author through to date of access and URL or DOI if it is a note from an online resource. Your regular notes can follow the first bibliographic note.

Generally, the notes you are writing will be one of three kinds (aside from the bibliographic). They perform, respectively, the functions of *quoting, paraphrasing,* and *summarizing.*

1. *Quotation.* When you quote a passage, you copy it word for word, placing quotation marks around it to remind you that it is a quotation. If there is a page break in your quotation, it should show in the pagination; if not, show it by placing a slash between the word ending one page and the word starting the next.

2. *Paraphrase.* The paraphrase note is often the longest note you write. It is roughly the length of the source you are paraphrasing but is written in your own words. You should use this kind of note sparingly because of the time it takes to compose.

3. *Summary.* This is the most condensed kind of note you write and the basic workhorse of note-taking. A summary note is written in your own words and is no more than thirty percent of the length of the original passage you are working on. For more on summarizing, see Chapter 8.

Each of these three kinds of notes should record the pages or location of the original text from which you made the note. If you use any of these notes in your finished paper, you have to acknowledge their source in a citation.

17-a Outlining

Research papers are extended essays. As such, formal prewriting activities, such as outlining, are useful in organizing your material before you start drafting. Once you have done the majority of your research, you will have a significant store of notes, thoughts, quotations, website references, and so on. Setting yourself the task of writing an outline for your paper will signal the end of the prewriting phase and the advent of the drafting stage.

You can decide if you want to attempt the most formal of outlines, the sentence outline, or whether a topical or phrasal outline will be sufficient. However, the discipline of writing this outline will force you to think about the different parts of your essay and how they interact. And that's a key step in the shift from amassing material to actually writing. For more information on outlining, refer to 1-e.

17-b Segmenting

In this simple technique, also known as *sectioning*, you settle for a general map. You sketch only the major segments of your project. Once you do this, you assemble your notes under the appropriate segment headings and begin to write.

One of the advantages of segmenting is that it allows you to tackle a manageable element immediately and not be intimidated by the size of your task. After you create your general map and assemble all your information under the appropriate headings, you can start writing about whichever segment you want.

17-c Writing a Draft Introduction

Some writers like to tackle the introduction first; others write it last. If you prefer to start with your introduction, don't aim for a polished version at this stage. Writers who try to perfect their introduction before they move on to other drafting tasks often find themselves afflicted with writer's block. Remember that all you need is a base from which to start. You can revise later.

17-d Integrating Quotations

SIGNAL PHRASES

Prose quotations of fewer than five typed lines in your essay (MLA style), fewer than forty words (APA style), or fewer than one hundred words (Chicago style) need to be worked skillfully into the text. A quotation that is dropped abruptly into the text will have a jarring effect.

To smooth the transition between text and quotation, preface the quotation with a signal phrase or integrate the quotation fully with your text.

In the following illustrations, you will see both MLA and APA citation styles given in the first example; they are then alternated in successive examples. The main difference between the two styles is the attachment of a date of publication to the author's name and the use of *p.* to signify page number in APA style.

Quotation with Signal Phrase

> Cultural factors played a major role in Japan's post-1945 economic recovery. According to Kennedy, "There was social ethos in favor of hard work . . ." (417).*

NOTE: Signal phrases should be used to introduce paraphrases and summaries as well.

Another common signal phrase consists of the author of the cited source and a verb that prepares readers for the quotation.

> Kennedy (1987) notes that "there was social ethos in favor of hard work . . ." (p. 417).*

NOTE: The preceding quotation begins with a lowercase letter (even though the original quotation begins with a capital letter) because a quotation introduced by the signal-phrase construction *Author + verb* is an essential syntactic part of the sentence. APA and Chicago style permit this silent change in the initial capital; MLA style does not.

The word *As*, the author's name, and an appropriate verb may also be used. This signal-phrase construction, like the *According to + author* construction, is set off with a comma.

---

*From *The Rise and Fall of the Great Powers*, by Paul Kennedy, copyright © 1987 by Paul Kennedy.

As Kennedy points out, "There was social ethos in favor of hard work . . ." (417).*

NOTE: A quotation introduced by the signal-phrase constructions *According to + author* or *As + author + verb* retains the initial capital letter because it is modified by, but is not an essential syntactic part of, the rest of the sentence.

If the quotation is not an independent clause but is instead a word, phrase, or dependent clause, you need to weave the quotation into your own sentence.

Kennedy (1987) draws a vivid contrast between Japan's tradition of government intervention in the economy and "the American laissez-faire approach" (p. 417).*

If there is a quotation within the quotation you wish to use, enclose the interior quotation in single quotation marks.

Kennedy offers a variety of explanations for the "'Japanese miracle'" that shaped the economy in the post-1945 period (417).*

For more information about punctuation with quotations, see 51-a and 51-b.

VERBS IN SIGNAL PHRASES

The verb you use in an *Author + verb* or an *As + author + verb* signal-phrase construction provides readers with a sense of the source's purpose. For example, *reports* suggests an attempt to inform, while *argues* suggests an attempt to persuade. Following is a list of verbs commonly found in both *Author + verb* and *As + author + verb* signal-phrase constructions.

acknowledges	contends	points out
admits	declares	recommends
advises	explains	reflects
argues	implies	remarks
asserts	indicates	says
claims	maintains	states
comments	notes	suggests
confirms	observes	writes

SIGNAL STATEMENTS

If you wish to provide more information than can be accommodated in a signal phrase, you may instead use a

---

*From *The Rise and Fall of the Great Powers*, by Paul Kennedy, copyright © 1987 by Paul Kennedy.

signal statement. If the statement is an independent clause, it is separated from the quotation by a colon.

[APA style] Cultural factors played a major role in Japan's post-1945 economic recovery. Kennedy (1987) comments on Japanese attitudes to work: "There was social ethos in favor of hard work . . ." (p. 417).*

Signal statements are frequently used to introduce *long quotations,* prose quotations of more than four lines (MLA style), forty words or more (APA style), or one hundred words or more (Chicago style).

[MLA style] Kennedy identifies the economic challenges Japan faced and the principal factors that enabled it to stage its dramatic post-1945 economic recovery:

> Although badly damaged by the 1937–1945 war, and cut off from its traditional markets and suppliers, it possessed an industrial infrastructure which could be repaired and a talented, well-educated, and socially cohesive population whose determination to improve themselves could now be channeled into peaceful commercial pursuits. (416–17)*

BRACKETS AND ELLIPSES

You can use square brackets and/or ellipses to make a quotation fit grammatically into your own sentence. An excess of ellipsis dots and brackets in the same passage makes for difficult reading, so use these marks of punctuation sparingly.

[MLA style] According to Kennedy, Japan's "fanatical belief in achieving the highest levels of quality control . . . [and] the national commitment to vigorous, high-level standards of universal education" were driving forces in the country's economic transformation (417).*

For further information about brackets and ellipses, see Chapters 55 and 57.

———
*From *The Rise and Fall of the Great Powers,* by Paul Kennedy, copyright © 1987 by Paul Kennedy.

It is essential that you set your first draft aside for a few days before you try to edit it. Imposing this break allows you to gain a critical perspective on your essay. It also gives you an opportunity to review in your mind what you have written.

Revising an essay is a daunting task. You can make the revising process more manageable if you focus on one facet of your essay at a time. To achieve this focus, you can make use of the four editing sweeps introduced in Chapter 5.

18-a Checking Your Formatting

In the proofreading sweep, also check for formatting errors. Specifically, check the following basic format requirements:

- separate title page or necessary information on the first page
- pagination in top right-hand corner of each page except a separate title page
- indented paragraphs
- aligned left margin
- double-spacing throughout, except for Chicago-style block quotations (single-space)
- correct parenthetical referencing
- correct quotation formats
- correct documentation style in Works Cited, References list, or Bibliography

Documentation

Different academic disciplines use different systems of documentation. The Modern Language Association (MLA) style, presented in the *MLA Handbook for Writers of Research Papers,* is used throughout the humanities. The American Psychological Association (APA) style, contained in the *Publication Manual of the American Psychological Association,* is followed by writers and students in the social sciences. The *Chicago Manual of Style* is the format recommended for history papers and is sometimes employed in other disciplines. The Council of Science Editors (CSE) style, presented in *Scientific Style and Format,* is the standard reference style for those in the scientific community. (Bibliographical information for the MLA, APA, Chicago, and CSE titles, and for style manuals used in a variety of disciplines, is provided in Table 19-1.)

TABLE 19-1 Style Manuals: Selected Disciplines

CHEMISTRY

Coghill, Anne M., and Lorrin R. Garson., ed. *The ACS Style Guide: Effective Communication of Scientific Information*. 3rd ed. Washington, DC: American Chemical Society, 2006.

GOVERNMENT

Canada. Public Works and Government Services Canada. Translation Bureau. *The Canadian Style: A Guide to Writing and Editing*. 2nd ed. Toronto: Dundurn Press, 1997.

HUMANITIES

Modern Language Association of America. *MLA Handbook for Writers of Research Papers*. 7th ed. New York: Modern Language Association of America, 2009.

HUMANITIES, NATURAL AND SOCIAL SCIENCES

The Chicago Manual of Style. 16th ed. Chicago: University of Chicago Press, 2010.

HUMANITIES AND SCIENCES: ONLINE STYLE

Walker, Janice R., and Todd Taylor. *Columbia Guide to Online Style*. 2nd ed. New York: Columbia University Press, 2006.

JOURNALISM

McCarten, James, ed. *The Canadian Press Stylebook: A Guide for Writers and Editors*. 17th ed. Toronto: Canadian Press, 2013.

McFarlane, J. A., and Warren Clements. *The Globe and Mail Style Book: A Guide to Language and Usage*. 9th ed. Toronto: McClelland and Stewart, 2003. (online searchable site only)

TABLE 19-1 Style Manuals: Selected Disciplines *(continued)*

LAW

Canadian Guide to Uniform Legal Citation. 7th ed. Toronto: Carswell, 2010.

Yogis, John A., et al. *Legal Writing and Research Manual*. 7th ed. Markham, ON: Butterworths, 2012.

MEDICINE

Iverson, Cheryl, et al. *AMA Manual of Style: A Guide for Authors and Editors*. 10th ed. New York: Oxford University Press, 2007.

MUSIC

Holomon, D. Kern. *Writing about Music: A Style Sheet from the Editors of 19th-Century Music*. Berkeley: University of California Press, 1988.

PHYSICS

American Institute of Physics. *AIP Style Manual*. 4th ed. New York: AIP, 1990. (out of print but available online)

SCIENCE

Style Manual Committee, Council of Science Editors. *Scientific Style and Format: The CSE Manual for Authors, Editors, and Publishers*. 7th ed. Reston, VA: Council of Science Editors with Rockefeller University Press, 2006.

SOCIAL SCIENCES

American Psychological Association. *Publication Manual of the American Psychological Association*. 6th ed. Washington, DC: APA, 2010.

The following examples of book, journal, and newspaper reference entries illustrate the basic differences among MLA, APA, and Chicago styles of documentation.

BOOK

Chao, Lien, and Jim Wong-Chu, eds. *Strike the Wok: An Anthology of Contemporary Chinese Canadian Fiction*. Toronto: TSAR, 2003. Print. [MLA]

Chao, L., & Wong-Chu J. (Eds.). (2003). *Strike the wok: An anthology of contemporary Chinese Canadian fiction*. Toronto, ON: TSAR. [APA]

Chao, Lien, and Jim Wong-Chu, eds. *Strike the Wok: An Anthology of Contemporary Chinese Canadian Fiction*. Toronto: TSAR, 2003. [Chicago]

JOURNAL ARTICLE

Hoben, Allan, and Robert William Hefner. "The Integrative Revolution Revisited." *World Development* 19.1 (1991): 17-30. Print. [MLA]

Hoben, A., & Hefner, R. W. (1991). The integrative revolution revisited. *World Development, 19*(1), 17–30. [APA]

Hoben, Allan, and Robert William Hefner. "The Integrative Revolution Revisited." *World Development* 19, no. 1 (1991): 17–30. [Chicago]

NEWSPAPER

Rasbach, Noreen. "Investor Stereotypes: Do Women Really Do It Better?" *Globe and Mail* 16 Feb. 2008, BC ed.: B8. Print. [MLA]

Rasbach, N. (2008, February 16). Investor

stereotypes: Do women really do it better?

The Globe and Mail, p. B8. [APA]

Rasbach, Noreen. "Investor Stereotypes: Do

Women Really Do It Better?" *Globe and*

Mail, February 16, 2008, sec. B. [Chicago]

Chapters 20–22 describe these various styles of documentation in detail.

MLA STYLE 20

Be aware of the following changes in the 2009 seventh edition of the *MLA Handbook for Writers of Research Papers*:

- Titles of works, such as books, paintings, plays, films, or any other works that were underlined previously in MLA style are now italicized.
- MLA does not give guidance for the presentation, in handwritten copy in an exam or time-limited test, of titles of works, such as books or other complete works. In these situations, the MLA convention of underlining should apply.
- URLs for online material are generally omitted in works-cited entries.
- Each works-cited entry now requires that its medium be provided: Print, Web, CD, LP, Television, Radio, Film, DVD, Videocassette.

20-a Parenthetical References

In MLA style, a parenthetical reference identifies a source and refers readers to the full description of the source in the list of works cited. Following are some sample MLA-style parenthetical references.

Author and page (short quotation)   Prose quotations that run no more than four lines in your essay and poetry quotations that contain no more than three lines of poetry are integrated into the text and enclosed in double quotation marks. The author's name need not appear in the parenthetical reference if it is included in the signal phrase. (For information about signal phrases, see Chapter 17.)

> Mark Kingwell defines happiness as "the possession of virtuous character and the performance of virtuous action" (327).

Author and page (long quotation)   Poetry quotations that include more than three lines of poetry and prose quotations that run more than four lines are set off from the text by indenting one inch (2.5 cm) from the left margin. Block quotations are not enclosed in quotation marks.

Author of more than one source   If the list of works cited contains more than one work by the same author, name the title in the parenthetical reference or in the text: (Shields, *Larry's Party* 160).

Two or three authors   If the source has two or three authors, include them in the parenthetical reference or name them in the text: (Abella and Troper xxii).

More than three authors   If the source has more than three authors, include in the text or parenthetical reference only the name of the first author followed by *et al.* ("and others"), without italics: (Simpson et al. 45).

Unidentified author   If the name of the author is unknown, either use the source's full title in the text or use the first two or three words of the title in the parenthetical reference: ("Poverty Trap" 28).

Corporate author   Place the names of corporate bodies in the parenthetical reference or in the text. (The preferred placement for long names is in the text.) In the parenthetical reference, shorten words that are commonly abbreviated: (Natl. Research Council 36).

Authors with the same last name   If the works-cited list contains works by two or more authors with the same last name, include the first initial in the parenthetical reference: (J. Smith 13); (D. Smith 45-49).

If the initial is shared, write the first name in full.

Multi-volume work   If your essay cites more than one volume of a multivolume work, include the volume number in the parenthetical reference. Note that a colon and a space separate the volume and page numbers.

> In her diary, Virginia Woolf expressed her
> reservations about *Ulysses* (2: 199–200).

Literary works   For most contemporary literary works, the treatment of references is simple, with the page number being the minimum information you need in a parenthetical citation for a prose work and the line number or numbers for a poem.

> **CONTEMPORARY NOVEL [page number]:** (257).

CONTEMPORARY PLAY
Contemporary plays do not, as a rule, use the convention of listing the line numbers for an act. Some also do not break acts down into scenes in the way that classical plays do. If you are faced with a play that does not use the conventions of act/scene/line, use a page number for your reference.

> **CONTEMPORARY POEM [line number or numbers]:** (2-3).

MLA suggests that you include either the word *line* or *lines* before the number reference the first time you make a parenthetical line reference, so your reader knows the reference is to line numbers (lines 4-5). Subsequent references need only include the line numbers (7-8).

When citing literary works that are available in several editions, help readers locate the passage by providing more than just the page number.

For a classic prose work, follow the page number with the chapter or part number: (Lawrence 532; ch. 30).

For a classic verse play, include the act, scene, and line numbers in the parenthetical reference. Use arabic numerals (Shakespeare 5.3.244-45) for the act and scene unless roman numerals (V.iii.244-45) are preferred by your instructor.

NOTE: If you are using an edition of a play that numbers the lines by page, ask your instructor if he or she wants you to include page numbers in the citations.

Indirect quotation   Use the abbreviation *qtd. in* to indicate that you are using someone else's report of a writer's or speaker's words: (qtd. in Kingwell 14).

Parenthetical references for online material   MLA states that parenthetical references for material from the Web should follow the same format as references for any other material. You should cite the page number of a Web source if it has page numbers. If the source does not have page numbers but numbers the paragraphs, you may cite the paragraph number. Otherwise, you should cite the title and list the source in your works-cited list at the end of your paper.

ONLINE DICTIONARY DEFINITION
If you use a specific definition from an online dictionary, place the word you have defined in a parenthetical reference and follow it with the abbreviation "def." and the number or letter the dictionary placed beside that specific definition: ("Two Bits," def. 1). As well, write a citation for the dictionary entry in your works-cited list.

20-b List of Works Cited

The list of works cited, which starts on a separate page at the end of the essay, contains complete bibliographical information for all the sources cited in the text. When constructing a works-cited list, follow these guidelines:

- Start the list on a separate page and title the list *Works Cited*.
- Centre the title an inch (2.5 cm) from the top of the page.
- Arrange the list *alphabetically* by the surnames of the authors or editors.
- If a work has no author or editor, alphabetize it according to the first word of its title. If the title's first word is *a, an,* or *the*, use the second word to determine placement.
- Do not indent the first line of each entry in the works-cited list. Indent subsequent lines a half-inch (or 1.25 cm). This format, called a *hanging indent*, makes the authors' surnames stand out for easy reference. (If your word processor has one, use the hanging-indent feature to format entries.)
- Double-space throughout the list.
- Italicize the title of a work unless it is part of a whole.

For a sample list of works cited, see page 117. Following are some sample works-cited entries.

BOOKS AND OTHER NON-PERIODICAL WORKS

One author You will find in a book's title and copyright pages the three basic units of a book entry: (1) author; (2) title; and (3) place of publication, publisher, year of publication. MLA also requires a fourth: medium. Use a shortened form of the publisher's name (for example, *Scribner's* for *Charles Scribner's Sons; Norton* for *W.W. Norton and Co., Inc.; Oxford UP* for *Oxford University Press;* or *Simon* for *Simon and Schuster, Inc.*).

Sakamoto, Kerri. *The Electrical Field*. Toronto: Knopf, 1998. Print.

Two or three authors Name the authors according to the order in which they appear on the title page. Invert the name of the first author so that the surname comes first. Separate the authors' names with commas.

> McNaught, Kenneth, and David Bercuson. *The*
>
> *Winnipeg General Strike*. Don Mills:
>
> Longman, 1974. Print.

More than three authors Name only the first author listed on the title page, and follow the name with a comma and *et al.* ("and others").

> Betcherman, G., et al. *The Canadian Workplace in*
>
> *Transition*. Kingston: IRC, 1994. Print.

Author with an editor After the author and the title, write the abbreviation *Ed.* ("Edited by") followed by the name of the editor.

> McClelland, Jack. *Imagining Canadian Literature:*
>
> *The Selected Letters of Jack McClelland*. Ed.
>
> Sam Solecki. Toronto: Key Porter, 1998. Print.

Corporate author Begin the entry with the corporate author's name, even if it is the name of the publisher as well.

> Canadian Museum of Civilization. *In the Shadow*
>
> *of the Sun: Perspectives on Contemporary*
>
> *Native Art*. Hull: Canadian Museum of
>
> Civilization, 1993. Print.

Unidentified author   Begin the entry with the title. Remember that titles are alphabetized by the first word other than *a, an,* or *the.*

> *The International Guide to English Language*
>
> > *Programs,* 1998. Victoria: EI Educ. Intl., 1997.
> >
> > Print.

More than one work by the same author   If your works-cited list contains two or more works by the same author, name the author only in the first entry. Begin subsequent entries with three hyphens followed by a period. List the entries alphabetically by title.

> Boyden, Joseph. *Three Day Road.* Toronto:
>
> > Viking-Penguin, 2005. Print.
>
> ———. *Through Black Spruce.* Toronto:
>
> > Viking-Penguin, 2008. Print.

Editor   Follow the name or names with the abbreviations *ed.* ("editor") or *eds.* ("editors").

> Heron, Craig, ed. *The Worker's Revolt in Canada,*
>
> > *1917-1925.* Toronto: U of Toronto P, 1998.
> >
> > Print.

Translation   Begin the entry with the author's name. After the title, write the abbreviation *Trans.* ("Translated by") and follow the abbreviation with the name of the translator.

> Carrier, Roch. *Prayers of a Young Man*. Trans.
>
> Sheila Fischman. Toronto: Penguin, 1999.
>
> Print.

Edition other than the first   If a book's title page indicates a later edition of the book, name the edition, in abbreviated form, after the title in your entry. An edition may be identified by number (*2nd ed., 3rd ed.,* etc.), by year (e.g., *2009 ed.*), or by name (*Rev. ed.* for "Revised Edition").

> Siegel, Arthur. *Politics and the Media in Canada*.
>
> 2nd ed. Whitby: McGraw, 1996. Print.

Multi-volume work   If you are citing two or more volumes of a multi-volume work, indicate (using the abbreviation *vols.*) the total number of volumes before the publication information.

> Bell, Quentin. *Virginia Woolf: A Biography*. 2 vols.
>
> London: Hogarth, 1972. Print.

If your essay cites only one volume, write the volume number before the publication information and provide publication information only for that volume.

> Bloom, Harold, ed. *The Art of the Critic: Literary*
>
> *Theory and Criticism from the Greeks to the*
>
> *Present*. Vol. 9. New York: Chelsea, 1989. Print.

Book in a series   If the book is part of a series, name the series (and any series number) after the medium of publication.

> Rogers, Edward S., and Donald B. Smith, eds.
>
> *Aboriginal Ontario: Historical Perspectives on*
>
> *the First Nations.* Toronto: Dundurn, 1994.
>
> Print. Ontario Historical Studies Ser.

Anthology or compilation   Follow the name of the editor or compiler with a comma and the abbreviation *ed.* or *comp.*

> Valleau, Al, and Jack Finnbogason, eds. *The*
>
> *Nelson Introduction to Literature.* 2nd ed.
>
> Toronto: Nelson, 2004. Print.

Selection in an anthology or compilation   Name the author of the selection, the selection title, and the title of the book. If the book has an editor or compiler, write the abbreviation *Ed.* ("Edited by") or *Comp.* ("Compiled by") after the title, followed by the person's name. Give the inclusive page numbers of the selection between the publication information and the medium of publication.

> Klein, A. M. "Haunted House." *The Collected Poems*
>
> *of A. M. Klein.* Comp. Miriam Waddington.
>
> Toronto: McGraw, 1974. 22-25. Print.

Multiple selections in an anthology or compilation   If you are citing two or more selections from the same collection, create an entry for the collection and cross-reference individual selections to the entry. For each selection, write the name or names of the author or authors and the title, the last name of the collection's editor or editors, and the inclusive page numbers.

> Ruffo, Armand Garnet. "Creating a Country." Valleau and Finnbogason 186-87.
>
> Valleau, Al, and Jack Finnbogason, eds. *The Nelson Introduction to Literature*. 2nd ed. Toronto: Nelson, 2004. Print.
>
> Wong-Chu, Jim. "old chinese cemetery kamloops july 1977." Valleau and Finnbogason 177-78.

Article in a dictionary or an encyclopedia Entries for information from dictionaries and encyclopedias are treated in the same way that you treat a poem or essay in an anthology. An entry for a word from a dictionary, however, does not need a reference to the dictionary's editor. An entry for an article in an encyclopedia will name the author of the article (if there is one), the article's title, the title of the encyclopedia, the edition number, the year of publication, and the medium of publication. Full publication information is not necessary if the reference book is well known. In this case, list the edition number and/or the year the edition was published.

> Doucett, Leonard E. "Drama in French." *The Canadian Encyclopedia*. 2000 ed. Print.
>
> "Zeugma." *The Oxford Encyclopedic English Dictionary*. 1991. Print.

Introduction, preface, foreword, or afterword Name the author of the element, identify the element, and then give the title of the book, the author (after the word *By*), and the editor (if there is one). Capitalize the name of the element but do not italicize it or enclose it in quotation marks. After the publication information, give the inclusive page numbers of the element and the medium of publication.

> Pollack, Zailig. Introduction. *Kaleidoscope:*
>
> *Selected Poems of P. K. Page*. By P. K. Page. Ed.
>
> Zailig Pollack. Erin, ON: Porcupine's Quill,
>
> 2010. 7-18. Print.

Book published before 1900 If the book you are citing was published before 1900, you may omit the name of the publisher. Use a comma, rather than a colon, between the place of publication and the date.

> James, William. *The Principles of Psychology*. New
>
> York, 1890. Print.

Republished book Add the original publication date after the title of the book. Then give the publication information for the edition you are citing.

> Mitchell, W. O. *The Vanishing Point*. 1973. Toronto:
>
> Macmillan, 1992. Print.

Publisher's imprint Imprints are special names under which publishers group their books. If the title page of a book you are citing includes the name of an imprint along with the name of the publisher, cite the imprint name followed by a hyphen and the publisher's name: Vintage-Random. NOTE: The publisher's name is the most critical element.

Pamphlet   Treat a pamphlet entry as you would a book entry.

> Leduc, Paul. *A Walking Tour of Old Montreal.*
>
>   Montreal: City of Montreal, 1973. Print.

Government publication   If the name of the document's author is not identified, begin with the name of the government that issued the document, followed by the name of the government agency.

> House of Commons. Standing Committee on
>
>   Citizenship and Immigration. *Reclaiming*
>
>   *Citizenship for Canadians: A Report on the Loss*
>
>   *of Canadian Citizenship.* Ottawa:
>
>   Communication Canada, 2007. Print.

Conference proceedings   List conference proceedings as you would books. After the title, add relevant information about the conference that is not included in the title. More and more conference proceedings are published online. If you are citing such proceedings, use the general guidelines for citing online material.

> Hiller, Steve, et al., eds. *Proceedings of the Library*
>
>   *Assessment Conference: Building Effective,*
>
>   *Sustainable, Practical Assessment.* 24-27 Oct.
>
>   2010, Baltimore, MD. Washington, DC:
>
>   Association of Research Libraries, 2011. Print.

Unpublished dissertation   Enclose the title in quotation marks. After the title, write the abbreviation *Diss.* followed by the name of the degree-granting body, the date, and the work's medium.

Campbell, Peter. "'Stalwarts of the Struggle':

Canadian Marxists of the Third Way,

1879-1939." Diss. Queen's U, 1991. Print.

Published dissertation   List published dissertations as you would books, but after the title add relevant information. If the dissertation was published privately, state *privately published* instead of a publisher's name.

Ames, Barbara. *Dreams and Painting: A Case*

Study of the Relationship between an Artist's

Dreams and Paintings. Diss. U of Virginia,

1978. Ann Arbor: UMI, 1979. Print.

ARTICLES AND OTHER PUBLICATIONS IN PERIODICALS

A periodical is a publication, such as a scholarly journal, a magazine, or a newspaper, that appears at regular intervals. When citing a publication in a periodical, follow these general guidelines:

- If an article in a periodical is not printed on consecutive pages, write the first number and a plus sign; for example, to cite the page numbers of an article that appears on pages 34-41 and 78-79, write *34+* (not *34-79*).

- When a title appears as part of a larger title, treat it as you would if it were by itself: "The Role of Fate in *Macbeth*" (an article about a play). For information about the treatment of titles of works in general, see 58-a.

- Abbreviate the names of months except for May, June, and July.

Article in a journal   For a periodical that numbers pages continuously within each annual volume, write the volume number (in arabic numerals) after the journal's title, followed by a period and the issue number (if available).

Wytenbroek, Lynn. "Harry Potter and the

Canadian Fantasy." *Canadian Literature*

186 (2005): 197-99. Print.

Article in a journal that uses only issue numbers   For a periodical that does not use volume numbers, cite only the issue number.

Powell, Martyn, and Malcolm Crook. "VII.

Eighteenth Century." *Annual Bulletin of*

Historical Literature 91 (2007): 83-103. Print.

Article in a monthly or bimonthly periodical   For a periodical that appears every month or every two months, give the month(s), year, and page numbers.

Le Guin, Ursula K. "Staying Awake: Notes on the

Alleged Decline of Reading." *Harper's* Feb.

2008: 33-38. Print.

Article in a weekly or biweekly periodical   For a periodical that appears every week or every two weeks, list the day, month, and year.

> Parks, Tim. "Hell and Back: A New Translation of
>
>   Dante's *Inferno.*" *New Yorker* 15 Jan. 2001: 84-
>
>   89. Print.

Article in a daily newspaper   List the author (if there is one), the article's title, the title of the newspaper, the complete date, the page number (including the section letter), and the medium of publication. Omit any initial article in the newspaper's name (*Vancouver Sun*, not *The Vancouver Sun*). If an edition is identified on the masthead, add a comma after the date and name the edition (e.g., *metro ed.*).

> Walton, Dawn. "The Inuit Cultural Matrix
>
>   Reloaded." *Globe and Mail* 15 Feb. 2008, BC
>
>   ed.: A3. Print.

Unidentified author in a periodical   Begin with the title if no author's name is given.

> "Christine Day: A Woman's Place Is at the Helm."
>
>   *Maclean's* 3 Mar. 2008: 65. Print.

Editorial or letter in a periodical   Add the word *Editorial* or *Letter* after the title (if any) or author's name.

> Abra, Eleanor, Letter *Maclean's* 6 May 2013: 7. Print.

Review

> Mack, Adrian. "Google, Our God Almighty." Rev. of
>
> *Google and the World Brain*, dir. Ben Lewis.
>
> *Georgia Straight* 2-9 May 2013: 59. Print.

OTHER SOURCES

Television or radio program   List the episode's title (if any), the title of the program or series (italicized), the network, the local station and city (if any), the broadcast date, and the medium of reception. Add other relevant information, such as narrator, performers, or director after the title.

> "Episode 105: The Wolf and the Lion." *Game of*
>
> *Thrones*. HBO Canada. 2 May 2011. Television.

Sound recording   Arrange the information in an entry (for example, composer, performer, conductor) according to your research emphasis. Include relevant information such as manufacturer and year of issue. Indicate the medium after the date of publication: *Audiocassette*, *Audiotape* (reel-to-reel tape), *CD*, or *LP* (long-playing record).

> Hansard, Glen, and Markéta Irglová. "Falling
>
> Slowly." *Once: Music from the Motion Picture*.
>
> Sony, 2007. CD.

Enclose the title of a specific song in quotation marks. Treat a spoken-word recording as you would a musical recording.

Film, videocassette, or DVD   List the title, the director, the distributor, the year of release, and the medium consulted. Other relevant information, such as the writer, producer, or performers, may be added. If you are citing a videocassette or DVD, cite the year of original release, the distributor, the year of release in that medium, and the medium.

> *Life of Pi*. Dir. Ang Lee. Perf. Suraj Sharma. 2012.
>
> 20th Century Fox, 2013. DVD.

If you wish to focus on a particular individual's work on the production, begin the entry with that person' name.

> Lawrence, Jennifer, perf. *Silver Linings Playbook*. Dir.
>
> David O. Russell. 2012. Weinstein, 2003. DVD.

Live performance   Begin with the title of the play, concert, ballet, or opera. Add relevant information, such as director, conductor, or performers, and conclude the entry with the location and date of the performance and an indication that you are citing a performance.

> *Transit of Venus*. By Victor Davies. Libretto by
>
> Maureen Hunter. Dir. Larry Desrochers.
>
> Cond. James Meena. Perf. Russell Braun,
>
> Judith Forst, Jean Stilwell, Monica Huisman,
>
> and Colin Ainsworth. Centennial Concert
>
> Hall, Winnipeg. 24 Nov. 2007. Performance.

Work of art   State the artist's name, the title of the work, the date and medium of composition, the name of the organization in which the work is housed, and the city. If the work is part of a private collection, follow the title with the name of the individual who owns it.

Colville, Alex. *Hound in Field*. 1958. Casein

tempera. National Gallery of Canada, Ottawa.

Map or chart   Treat a map or chart as you would a book with an unidentified author, but add the word *Map* or *Chart* after the title.

Newfoundland and Labrador. Map. Ottawa:

Natural Resources Canada, 2001. Print.

Interview   To cite a published interview or an interview broadcast on television or radio, begin with the name of the person interviewed and the title of the interview, if any, in quotation marks. Follow with the interviewer's name. Conclude with the appropriate bibliographical information and the medium of publication.

If the interview is untitled or has a title that does not indicate the nature of the source, use the descriptive identifier *Interview*. Add the interviewer's name if known and relevant.

Garneau, Marc. Interview by Shelagh Rogers.

Sounds Like Canada. CBC Radio One. 5 Oct.

2004. Radio.

If you conducted the interview, state the type of interview (*Personal interview, Telephone interview*).

Lecture, speech, address, or reading State the speaker's name, the title of the oral presentation (if known) in quotation marks, the sponsoring body (if any), and the location and date of the presentation. Conclude with an appropriate description (*Lecture, Address, Reading, Keynote speech,* etc.) to show the form of delivery.

> Yee, Paul. "Becoming a Writer." The Helen E.
> Stubbs Memorial Lectures. Osborne
> Collection of Early Children's Books, Lillian
> H. Smith Branch, Toronto Public Library,
> Toronto. 19 Oct. 2006. Lecture.

Personal communication To cite a letter you have received, begin with the sender's name. Then write the phrase *Letter to the author* followed by the date. Conclude with the medium: TS for typewritten; MS for handwritten (manuscript).

> Page, P. K. Letter to the author. 16 Apr. 1994. TS.

ELECTRONIC SOURCES

Electronic sources include CD-ROMs, email, software programs, websites, online databases, and information available using telnet, gopher, file transfer protocol (FTP), and other access modes. This section deals specifically with email, CD-ROMs and DVD-ROMs, and websites.

Electronic communication To cite electronic mail you have received, begin with the sender's name and, if there is one, the title (taken from the subject line). Then write the phrase *Message to the author* followed by the date and the medium of delivery (*Email*). If the email was to someone other than you, instead of writing *Message to the author*, write *Message to* plus the name of the recipient of the email.

Chiang, Valerie. "Re: Archetypes." Message to the
author. 7 Mar. 2001. Email.

WEB SOURCES

In its seventh edition (2009), the *MLA Handbook* stresses
that the referencing of electronic material should have the
same goal as the referencing of printed texts—the accurate identification of a text and how it may be located.
However, electronic texts have not arrived at a standard
format and are also less stable than printed texts.
Therefore, more information should be given for electronic than for printed texts. Specifically, MLA requires
that a citation or bibliographic entry for an electronic text
should include information about electronic publication
and access details.

By "access details," MLA now means the date you read
the electronic text. The previous edition of the *MLA
Handbook* required the inclusion of the URL for the text;
the seventh edition now recommends that the URL not be
included unless your instructor requires it or you are certain that your readers could not locate your resource
without having the URL. Of course, if you do include a
URL, it must be enclosed in angle brackets (< >) and
appear as the last element in the citation, and the URL
cannot be split between two lines unless you do so following a slash. Generally, however, MLA has concluded
that URLs have become too cumbersome and unstable to
be a useful part of works-cited list entries.

In summary, a works-cited reference for an electronic
source will add two areas of detail: the type of medium
(Web) where the source appears, and the date of access (the
date when you read or downloaded the source).

AUTHOR

Include the name or names of the author(s) of the text.
Use the name of a site if no individual author is identified;
if neither an author nor a site is named, use the name of
the site's sponsor.

TITLE

Include the title of the work, italicized. If it is a title of part
of a whole, present the title of the part in quotation marks

and italicize the title of the whole. If there is an editor, a compiler, or a translator, his or her name follows the title.

PUBLICATION DETAILS WHEN PRINTED VERSION AVAILABLE

If there is a printed version of the text, give the publication information for that version first.

PUBLICATION DETAILS FOR ELECTRONIC SOURCE

The publication details for the electronic source of the text follow the publication information for the printed version. These may include the title of the site, the name of an editor for the site (if one exists), the volume or issue number or other identifying details for an article from a journal, the date of the electronic publication or update (if one is given), the name of the service from which the text was taken, the name of the list or forum (if the text is drawn from such a source), the number of units in the text (if individual units, such as pages or paragraphs, are identified), and the name of any institution or organization acting as the site's publisher or sponsor (if not available, use *N.p.*).

> Chao, Lien. "Anthologizing the Collective: The
>
> Epic Struggles to Establish Chinese Canadian
>
> Literature in English." *Essays on Canadian*
>
> *Writing* 57 (1995): 145-61. *ProQuest.* Web. 20
>
> Apr. 2009.

The last two publication details required in the citation of an electronic source are

- the medium of publication (Web)
- the date that you visited the site and read or downloaded the text

Please consult the MLA site for updates on documenting electronic sources. The URL for the site is http://www.mla.org.

The following examples provide an overview of the more common electronic sources and how they would be cited on a works-cited page.

Scholarly project

> Jokinen, Anniina, ed. *Anthology of Middle English Literature (1350–1485)*. N.p., 5 Sept. 2000. Web. 13 Nov. 2004.

Document within a scholarly project

> Schiller, Friedrich. "The Sport of Destiny." Trans. Marian Klopfer. 1786. *Nineteenth-Century German Stories*. Ed. Robert Godwin-Jones. Foreign Lang. Dept., Virginia Commonwealth U, 1994. Web. 12 Jan. 2004.

Professional site

> Professional Association of Canadian Theatres. Home Page. Professional Association of Canadian Theatres, 2013. Web. 1 May 2013.

Personal site

> Rotenberg, Robert. "Biography." Home page. n.d. Web. 17 May 2013.

Book

The seventh edition of the MLA Handbook does not include the possibility that the online text may have a date when it was uploaded as well as when it was updated. Ask your instructor if you should include both the upload and update information.

> Montgomery, Lucy Maud. *Anne of the Island*.
>
>   1915. *Project Gutenberg*. Web. 1 Apr. 2013.

The above example is from a website that reproduces a book but does not give its original publication information. MLA suggests that if the site does give that information, it may be important to include it in your works-cited entry. If you do, you should include the information in this order: author's name, title of work, city of publication, publisher (if published after 1900), date of publication, title of website or database, medium of publication consulted (Web), and date of access.

> Babbage, Charles. *Passages from the Life of a*
>
>   *Philosopher*. London, 1864. *Online Books*
>
>   *Page*. N.p, n.d. Web. 24 Apr. 2009.

Article in an information database

> Hayne, David M., and Kathleen Kellett-Betsos.
>
>   "Canadian Literature: 1960 and Beyond."
>
>   *Encyclopedia Britannica Online*. Encyclopedia
>
>   Britannica, 2009. Web. 18 Jan. 2009.

Article in a journal

> Ward, Ian. "Shakespeare and the Politics of
>
>   Community." *Early Modern Literary Studies*
>
>   4.3 (1999): n. pag. Web. 3 Jan. 2004.

Article in a magazine

McLaren, Leah. "The Lost Generation of

Unvaccinated Kids." *Macleans.ca*. Maclean's

Magazine, 25 Apr. 2013. Web. 3 May 2013.

Article in a newspaper

Taylor, Kate. "NFB to Launch the Netflix of the

Documentary World." *Globe and Mail*. Globe

and Mail, 30 Apr. 2013. Web. 10 May 2013.

Material from a library subscription service As libraries move from subscribing to hard copies of periodicals, to utilizing library subscription services that allow users to access periodical articles electronically, works-cited entries for online service articles will become more prevalent. Although it is convenient for students to access articles electronically, citing the source of an article acquired online can be challenging.

The MLA guidelines for articles from databases simplify what was a complex issue. As MLA does not recommend that you include URLs with works-cited entries unless your instructor wants you to, after the information that would be needed for a print periodical, you need only add the title of the database (in italics), the fact that the material is from the Web (Web), and the date of access (day, month, and year).

Here is an example of a works-cited entry for an article from a database:

Kramer, Reinhold. "Nationalism, the West and

The Englishman's Boy." *Essays on Canadian

Writing* 67 (Spring 1999): 1-22. *ProQuest*.

Web. 20 Apr. 2009.

In summary, an entry for an article you obtained through a subscription service will include the author, title of essay, title of periodical, publishing details, pages (if not available, use *n. pag.*), database, medium of publication, and access date

Non-periodical publications: Wikis, blogs, course webpages, and other electronic sources   MLA describes how to set up an entry for material from a "non-periodical publication," and these guidelines can be adapted for citing material from a wiki, blog, or course webpage. The main elements are

- the author's name (or compiler, director, editor);
- the title of the work (in italics if the work stands alone, or in quotation marks if it is a part of a larger element);
- the title of the site, wiki, blog, or course webpage (in italics), if there is such a name;
- the version or edition, if known;
- the publisher or sponsor if there is one, or *N.p.* if one is not listed;
- the date of publication, if known, or *n.d.* if not;
- the medium (Web);
- the date of access.

> Buirs, Betty Anne. "The Thesis Statement—
>
> Narrowing the Topic." *Virtual Learning*
>
> *Centre.* The Learning Centre, Kwantlen
>
> Polytechnic U, 2009. Web. 17 Apr. 2009.

In most examples in the *MLA Handbook* itself, the elements that are listed are author, title, title of site, publisher or sponsor, date of publication, medium, and date of access. Many of MLA's examples exclude version or edition, publisher, sponsor or *N.p.*, and date of publication or *n.d.* If you are unsure of the format for an individual entry, see your instructor. You might also want to look at Columbia Online style, as it covers numerous online possibilities that MLA, APA, and Chicago do not comment on.

20-c MLA-Style Sample Essay

On the following pages you will find two parts of an MLA-style essay.[1] Format specifications are pointed out in the marginal notes.

---

[1] Adapted from an essay by Stacey Fruno, a student in an English literature class at Kwantlen Polytechnic University.

Fruno 1

Stacey Fruno ← *Author's name, instructor's name, course's name and section number, and date typed 1" (2.5 cm) from top of first page and flush with left margin*

Dr. Paul Tyndall

ENGL 3313

9 April 2013

If It's Not for You to Say …Who Is to Say It?

Power Dynamics and Language in ← *Title centred on page*

David Mamet's *Oleanna*

Paragraphs indented 1/2" (1.25 cm) → Like many other readers or viewers of David Mamet's *Oleanna*, I had a strong reaction to the ending of the play, and this reaction surprised me. I was happy, even excited, when John both verbally and physically assaulted Carol. This reaction was amplified when I viewed the 1994 movie, directed by Mamet himself. As a student, I am of course sometimes confused and anxious in regards to my classes. For this reason, I found myself empathizing with Carol here and there throughout Act 1. By the end, however, I thought to myself, "Thank goodness! Finally!" when John at last loses control and assaults Carol. As a female college student similar to Carol's age, in reality, I do not support the actions of the professor towards the student in the end of the play, but there is something so irritating, even threatening, about Carol's presence, that I felt the desire to hit her myself. So what is it about the play that garners such responses and transference of emotions that go as far to evoke a desire for violence in the readers or viewers? Why is it that even females have such distaste for Carol's character? Much attention has been directed towards the gender politics, but, if it were the gender struggle that was so volatile, would females

not support Carol at the end of the play in her
supposed "win" in her own gender war? The study
of reader responses and an examination of
performance interpretations help to demonstrate
the power of Mamet's language in the creation of
emotions in his viewers or readers. By examining
the power dynamics in *Oleanna* outside of (but not
completely ignoring) gender politics, analysis may
suggest that sexual hostility is not Carol's
motivation; rather, it becomes a tool in her struggle
for power.

Others have also perceived Carol in a negative
light as I did. In "Framing the Classroom: Pedagogy,
Power, *Oleanna*," Stanton B. Garner, Jr. employs
reader response criticism to explore the reactions of
his own students to the play, which they both read
and saw performed by "Clarence Brown Theatre
Company at the University of Tennessee" (Garner
42). The students' responses were violent and
jarring: "'In the end you want to be right up there
with John when he hits her'; 'Many times in the
performance, I just wanted to reach out and scream
and pull out Carol's hair myself'; 'I went into the
play hating Carol and came out ready to kill her'"
(45). Casual remarks online about the 1994 movie
included much of the same categorization of Carol:
"Obviously he hit his breaking point, and Carrol
got what she deserved" (Trekynoah). Surprisingly, it
is not just male students who side with John. One
of Garner's female students remarked, "After I saw
Oleanna performed, I sided with John because I felt
she had provoked John to 'sexually harass' her"

(46). I would suggest that, if there were any reason to side with Carol over John in the rightness of her gender politics, female students would be the viewers to connect with this aspect, but they don't. This suggests that there is much more to the conflict in this play than an exploration of gender battles.

Paragraphs indented 1/2" (1.25 cm) → This idea that Carol "deserves" the beating hinges on the first act. Whether the sexual suggestiveness is played up or down, it seems the audience will come to find that her accusations were exaggerated and false. In the Clarence Brown Theatre Company's production of *Oleanna*, "Carol flirted with John in the opening part of the first act, the director added a number of physical overtures on John's part," and Garner describes how "the issue of sexuality was foregrounded" (45). Despite the "physical overtures" in this production such as when John "put his hand inside the hole in her jeans" (47) that should have viewers become aggressive toward John, students still came out hating Carol, including female students. The film production differs in that Carol is essentially de-feminized through the costume choice, both in the first act where she is in a baggy shirt and jeans, and the second act where she appears in an ill-fitting masculine suit. It seems whether Carol is put in frumpy clothes and de-feminized, or wearing "cut-offs, [and a] skimpy shirt" (Garner 46), she is perceived in the same way. This suggests that it is not her appearance or gender that matters; rather it is her words, Mamet's words, which have such a volatile effect.

In "The Politics of Gender, Language and Hierarchy in Mamet's *Oleanna*," Christine MacLeod discusses how language is intricately related to power and how too much attention is given to the alleged anti-feminist ploy of the piece. There is an obvious imbalance between the number of readers/viewers who side with John over Carol, despite the fact that "Mamet himself insisted that *Oleanna* does not take sides" (201). MacLeod points out that "it is worth considering how much of this perceived imbalance actually stems from the text and how much from the variables of directorial judgement" (201). It would appear that, among my own cold read of the play, my reaction to the film version, and Garner's students' reader responses to both the script and the production, different "variables of directorial judgment" still result in similar responses. This suggests that the negative aspects of Carol's character lie in the script itself, not the interpretation.

. . . .
. . . .

It could be said that, since Carol is female and desires power over John, the play is ultimately about gender issues and anti-feminism; it is Carol's supposed "weaker" or lower position as a female that gives her the desire for power. I would argue that it is not her gender that is the driving force in her aggressive actions. Rather the accusations of sexual harassment and rape are " a matter of tactics, of deploying to best advantage the best available weapons" (MacLeod 207). As a student, she is already in a lower position than John and works to overturn his hierarchy. In Act 1, John's interruptions and control over language comes from his position as a teacher, not from his gender. As a university professor herself (and important to this point, a female), MacLeod found "that as a teacher—by virtue of academic status and a competence in certain privileged forms of discourse—I too could be and perhaps have been guilty of the same insensitivity towards students, the same arrogance and verbal aggression" (203). Similarly, when Carol is in power, she only uses rape and sexual harassment as a tool to advance herself against a male and a teacher, respectively against gender and power.

By the end of the play, we have witnessed John "trying to commandeer Carol's voice" (MacLeod 202) shift to Carol taking the words out of John's mouth: "Don't call your wife baby" (Mamet 79). John's reaction is to regain his power the only way he has left at his disposal: physical violence. Perhaps it is the threat of losing one's own voice that makes Carol's character so threatening to the viewer. The fact that what you say "can and will be used against you" is something that we might not think about on a daily basis, but it is always present. The same is to be said about the power dynamics that we may encounter on a daily basis. The theme of disruption of the power dynamics in *Oleanna* is unnerving to the viewer since the play posits that what you say can be used against you, and that the overwhelming desire for power and

sinister ways that can be used to overturn positions
of power hinges on mere words. Carol is hated, not
because of her abuse of power, but because of her
manipulation of both language and gender politics
to gain power. Language represents power to the
characters, but it also holds power over them. The
same can be said about real people, which is why
Mamet's language is so emotionally evocative.

Works Cited

Garner, Stanton B. "Framing the Classroom: Pedagogy, Power, *Oleanna*." *Theatre Topics* 10.1 (2000): 39-52. Web. 1 Apr. 2013.

Mamet, David. *Oleanna*. New York: First Vintage, 1992. Print.

MacLeod, Christine. "The Politics of Gender, Language and Hierarchy in Mamet's *Oleanna*." *Journal of American Studies* 29.2 (1995): 199-213. Web. 5 Apr. 2013.

Oleanna. Dir. David Mamet. MGM, 1994. *YouTube*. Web. 30 Mar. 2013.

"*Oleanna* Role Reversal." Muhlenberg College, 2005. *YouTube*. Web. 07 Apr. 2013.

Trekynoah. "*Oleanna*: 1 love this movie." *YouTube*. 8 Mar. 2013. Web. 6 Apr. 2013.

Works Cited typed, centred, 1" (2.5 cm) from top of page

First line flush left, subsequent lines indented 1/2" (1.25 cm)

21-a Parenthetical Citations

In APA style, a parenthetical citation in the text identifies the source of a borrowing and enables readers to locate the source in a list of references at the end of the essay. A typical parenthetical citation includes the author's name and the year of publication. (The inclusion of the date reflects the importance of currency of research in the social sciences.) Page numbers are usually provided only for direct quotations. Please note that the current *Publication Manual* includes Table 6.1 on p. 177. It shows light varients of "Basic Citation Style" and is a useful reference. Following are some sample APA citations.

Author and date   Place a comma between the author and the date in the parenthetical citation. If the author is named in the text, place the date immediately after the name.

> People with Type 0 blood are more likely to develop duodenal ulcers than people with Type A, B, or AB blood (Eisenberg, 1978).
>
> Eisenberg (1978) found that people with Type 0 blood are more likely to develop duodenal ulcers than people with Type A, B, or AB blood.

Author, date, and page (short quotation)   Quotations of fewer than forty words are integrated into the text and enclosed in double quotation marks. Note the use of the past tense *(reported)* in the text and the inclusion of the abbreviation *p.* before the page number in the parenthetical citation.

> As Schulsinger (1992) reported, "The greatest workplace stress occurs when jobs are high in stressors and low in controllability" (p. 56).

If the author's name does not appear in the signal phrase, place it in the parenthetical citation at the end of the quotation: (Schulsinger, 1978, p. 56).

Author, date, and page (long quotation)   Quotations of more than forty words are set off from the text by indenting five spaces from the left margin. Quotation marks are omitted. The parenthetical citation follows the period at the end of the quotation.

Two authors   If a work has two authors, use both names in all citations. Note the use of the ampersand (&) in the parenthetical citation and the spelled-out *and* in the text.

> The outcome measures used in the study have
>
> been criticized (Campbell & Tsuang, 2001).
>
> Campbell and Tsuang (2001) have criticized the
>
> outcome measures used in the study.

Three to five authors   If a work has three to five authors, list all their names in the text or the parenthetical citation the first time you cite the work: (Rosenthal, Kelly, Allen, & Santos, 1995).

In subsequent citations, use only the name of the first author followed by *et al.* ("and others"): Rosenthal et al. (1995) found that . . . .

Six or more authors   If a work has six or more authors, use only the first author's name followed by *et al.* in all citations, including the first.

Unidentified author   If the author's name is unknown, include in the parenthetical citation the work's title and the year of publication: ("Treatment Evaluation," 1997).

Corporate author   Spell out the name of a corporate body in the text.

> The Consensus Development Panel (2009)
>
> concluded . . . .

If the corporate body has a long and cumbersome name, spell out the name in the first parenthetical citation, followed by an abbreviation in brackets. In subsequent citations, use only the abbreviation.

Authors with the same surname If your reference list contains works by two or more primary authors with the same last name, include the first author's initials in all citations.

More than one work in parentheses Works by different authors who appear in the same parenthetical citation are listed in alphabetical order by the first author's surname and separated by semicolons.

> (Braun, 1991; Langer et al., 1986; Wilkinson, 2000)

Two or more works by the same author are arranged by date of publication and separated by commas: (Kamani, 1994, 1999, 2001).

Personal communication Identify personal communications, such as letters and memos, in the text rather than in the list of references. Cite the sender's initials and surname, the words *personal communication*, and the date.

> (C. Misaka, personal communication, February
>
> 26, 2001)

Online references to specific parts of a source With an online source, if there is no page number, APA suggests you indicate the paragraph number for the source, using "para." If neither the page number nor the paragraph number is supplied, you should cite the section heading as in the examples below.

(Statistics Canada, 2001, para. 2)

(Public Health Agency of Canada, 2004, Reported AIDS cases and ethnicity: A balance of changing proportions)

21-b Content Footnotes

A content footnote is an optional element that expands on substantive information in the text. Content footnotes should not be used for complex or unnecessary information. APA style recommends that a content footnote convey no more than one idea.

A superscript Arabic numeral indicates the content footnote's position in the text. The first line of a footnote is indented like the first line of a paragraph. Footnotes are typed (double-spaced) in the order of their appearance in the essay. Put them on a separate page after the references.

21-c List of References

In APA style, the list of references provides bibliographical information for an essay's parenthetical citations. The reference list, titled *References*, starts on a separate page at the end of the essay. Entries in a reference list are alphabetically arranged by the surnames of the authors or editors. Reference entries that lack authors or editors are alphabetized by the first word of the title, excluding *a, an,* or *the*. Double-spacing is used between and within entries throughout the list.

For individual reference entries, APA requires the use of a hanging-indent style.

American Psychological Association. (2010).

Publication manual of the American

Psychological Association. 6th ed. Washington,

DC: Author.

Listed below are APA guidelines for creating reference entries, followed by sample entries for various types of sources. For a sample APA reference list, see page 138.

1. Invert authors' names that precede titles; do not invert authors' names that follow titles. Use initials instead of first and middle names in all authors' names. To reference a work by two authors, cite both names. For three to seven authors, include all names. An ampersand appears before the final author's name. For eight or more authors, list the first six authors, followed by an ellipsis and the name of the last author. In all cases, authors' names are separated with commas.

2. Follow the last author's name with the date of publication (in parentheses). If no date is available, write in its place *n.d.* (in parentheses).

3. Italicize titles and subtitles of books (include the period following the title in italics). Capitalize only the first word of the title and any subtitle, along with all proper nouns.

4. Italicize titles and volume numbers of periodicals (include in the italicizing the comma following the title or volume number). For journal titles, capitalize the first word and all other words except articles, conjunctions, and prepositions of fewer than four letters.

5. Do not enclose titles of articles in quotation marks. Capitalize only the first word of the article's title and any subtitle, along with all proper nouns.

6. Include any initial article in the names of newspapers *(The Globe and Mail,* not *Globe and Mail).*

7. Use the abbreviation *p.* or *pp.* before page numbers of newspaper articles and selections in edited books. Do not use the abbreviation before page numbers in journals, magazines, and newsletters.

8. Omit from the names of publishers words that are not required to identify the publisher *(Wiley,* not *John Wiley & Sons).* However, retain the words *Books* and *Press* and spell out the names of university presses. Omit business abbreviations such as *Co., Ltd.,* and *Inc.* If the author named at the start of the entry is the publisher as well, write the word *Author,* not the author/publisher's name, in the publication information element.

9. Because the DOI (digital object identifier) of an article remains the same for print publication or electronic (the DOI is a unique number for that article, regardless of the medium of publication), APA format recommends including the DOI, if one has been assigned to the source, even if you're referencing the print version. The DOI comes last in the journal article entry, after the page numbers.

ITALICS/UNDERLINING AND DASHES

APA style uses italics for titles of works; for periodicals, the title includes the volume number.

In APA-style essays, two hyphens (--) can be used to indicate a dash. There is no space before, between, or after the hyphens.

BOOKS AND OTHER NON-PERIODICAL WORKS

One author

Kahneman, D. (2011). *Thinking, fast and slow.*

Scarborough, ON: Doubleday Canada.

Two or more authors

Burtch, B., & Larsen, N. (2006). *Law in society: Canadian readings*. Toronto, ON: Nelson.

Corporate author

Canadian Pharmaceutical Association. (2008). *Compendium of pharmaceuticals and specialties (Canada)*. Ottawa, ON: Author.

Unidentified author

Encyclopedia of African peoples. (2000). New York, NY: Facts On File.

Order of two or more works by the same author

Sacks, O. (1995). *An anthropologist on Mars*. New York, NY: Knopf.

Sacks, O. (2012). *Hallucinations*. New York, NY: Knopf.

Order, same author with same publication date

Eichler, M. (1988a). *Families in Canada today: Recent changes and their policy consequences.* Toronto, ON: Gage.

Eichler, M. (1988b). *Nonsexist research methods: A practical guide.* Boston, MA: Allen & Unwin.

Editor

Caruth, C. (Ed.). (1995). *Trauma: Explorations in memory.* Baltimore, MD: Johns Hopkins University Press.

Edition other than the first

Morrison, K. (2006). *Marx, Durkheim, Weber: Formations of modern social thought* (2nd ed.). Thousand Oaks, CA: Sage.

Selection in an edited book

Christie, G. (2007). Police-government relations in the context of state-Aboriginal relations. In M. Beare & T. Murray (Eds.), *Police and government relations: Who's calling the shots?* (pp. 147–172, 176–182). Toronto, ON: University of Toronto Press.

Entry in an encyclopedia or dictionary

Swanson, P. (2006). Habitat for humanity. In
Encyclopedia of world poverty (Vol. 2, pp.
455–456). Thousand Oaks, CA: Sage.

Government publication

Abbott, K. (2003). *Urban Aboriginal women in
British Columbia and the impacts of the
matrimonial real property regime* (Catalogue
No. R2-271/2003E). Ottawa, ON: Indian and
Northern Affairs.

Published contribution to a symposium

Wheeler, D. (1991). Creating culturally specific AIDS
interventions: An example of the ethnographic
approach to program evaluation. In K. J. Jaros
& G. C. St. Denis (Eds.), *Proceedings of the 1991
Public Health Social Work Institute* (pp. 36–54).
Pittsburgh: University of Pittsburgh.

PERIODICALS

Article in a journal paginated by volume

Gionet, L. (2009, Summer). Métis in Canada:
Select findings of the 2006 census. *Canadian
Social Trends, 87,* 22–25.

Article in a journal paginated by issue

Atkins, C. (2006). A cripple at a rich man's gate: A comparison of disability. *Canadian Journal of Law and Society, 21*(2), 87–111.

Article in a magazine

Casey, A. (2008, January/February). Carbon cemetery. *Canadian Geographic, 128*(1), 56–66.

For a biweekly or weekly magazine, add the correct day after the month.

Article in a daily newspaper

Carmichael, K. (2008, March 11). Kill RESP bill or go to polls, Liberals told. *The Globe and Mail,* pp. A1, A9.

Letter to the editor

Shams, Z. (2001, January 11). Women in Iran [Letter to the editor]. *The Globe and Mail,* p. A12.

Review

Platt, J. (2008, Winter). [Review of the book *Family and community in Ireland,* by C. M. Arensberg and S. T. Kimball]. *Journal of the History of the Behavioural Sciences, 41*(1), 77.

ELECTRONIC SOURCES

The sixth edition of the *Publication Manual of the American Psychological Association* reminds writers of papers to do two things when citing an electronic work:

- Provide the DOI, or, where no DOI has been assigned, the URL for the home page of the journal, or of the publisher of the book or report.

- Take special pains to provide accurate and reliable locator information (DOIs, URLs).

The sixth edition has also withdrawn the previous APA requirement that URLs be written on a single line to avoid confusion, using a reduced font, if necessary, to provide that address. Writers can now run an address into a second or even a third line, as long as they ensure that the break between lines comes only before most punctuation.

Finally, the sixth edition recommends certain other details for the citation of electronic texts, including the following:

- If you used the electronic version of a print book, APA instructs you to add the electronic version name [Adobe Digital Editions version] after the book's title before the web address. APA acknowledges that the format of a reference for a journal article automatically indicates whether the print or web version was used.

- If you are using material taken from a private database, or archival material found only in such sources as ERIC or JSTOR, cite the homepage of that database. Only these types of databases need URLs as other URLs are unstable or unreliable indicators of an article's location.

- APA does not require a date of retrieval for electronic sources unless the material is from a wiki or some other unstable source in which the material is subject to change.

- APA now includes Internet message boards, electronic mailing lists, and online communities as sources that need to be cited. To cite such sources, follow the standard APA entry format. If the author is named, follow standard APA style; if the author uses a screen name only, use that name in place of the author's name. Include the date of the posting of the message after the author's name, the subject line, or thread name, and then, in brackets, the type of source you are citing.

Dhillon, M. (2010, February 4). Re: Discussion of

societal norms [Online forum comment].

Retrieved from http://psychdiscussiongroup

/psychstudentonline/2010/02/societalnorms

/Webblog/topic_ten_discussion

Please consult the APA website for current information at http://www.apastyle.org.

Book

Gray, H. (2000). *Anatomy of the human body.*

Retrieved from http://www.bartleby.com/107/

(Original work published 1918).

Article in a journal

ARTICLE FOUND ONLY IN AN ONLINE SOURCE

Berg, M., & Seeber, B. (2013). The slow professor:

Challenging the culture of speed in the

academy. *Transformative Dialogues, 6*(2), 1–7.

Retrieved from http://kwantlen.ca/TD

/TD.6.3/TD.6.3.5 _Berg&Seeber

_Slow_Professor.pdf

ARTICLE IN A JOURNAL WITH DOI REFERENCE

International publishers developed the DOI (Digital Object Identifier) system in response to the problem of unstable URLs for online material. You will often find DOIs in the electronic catalogue entry for an article; many publishers also print them on the first page of an article. The DOI may sometimes be under a button with a title like *Article* or *CrossRef*. If there is a DOI, use it and omit the URL. Simply add "doi:" and the DOI alpha-numeric string to the end of your entry (there is no space after the colon). Generally, when a DOI string runs to a second line, you break the first line before a punctuation mark and start the second line with the punctuation. There is no period after a DOI.

Archambault, I., Janosz, M., Morizot, J., & Pagani, L. (2009). Adolescent behavioral, affective, and cognitive engagement in school: Relationship to dropout. *Journal of School Health, 79*(9), 408–415. doi:10.1111/j.1746-1561.2009.00428.x

Article in a magazine

Millar, A. (2008, March 18). Facebook cheating scandal nothing new. *Maclean's.* Retrieved from http://oncampus.macleans.ca/education/2008/03/18/facebook-cheating-scandal-nothing-new/

Article with no author and no date Begin the reference with the title if there is no author.

Sociology in the higher education of women. (n.d.). Retrieved from http://www.theatlantic.com/doc/189211/womens-education9bg

Article in a newspaper

Chase, S., Curry, B., & Leblanc, D. (2013, May 22).

RCMP now looking into Senate expenses

scandal. *The Globe and Mail*. Retrieved from

http://www.theglobeandmail.com

Review

Jinje, S. (2013, April). [Review of the book *The*

Great Black North: Contemporary African

Canadian Poetry]. *Quill and Quire*. Retrieved

from http://www.quillandquire.com

Entry in an encyclopedia

Differential psychology. (2013). *Encyclopedia*

Britannica Online. Retrieved from

http://members.eb .com/bol/topic?eu=30910

&sctn=1

Blogs, wikis, podcasts

Entries for blogs, wikis, podcasts, and similar online forums follow the standard APA format:

- Last name followed by initial of first (if there is only a screen name, use the screen name in place of the name);
- The date of the posting in parentheses (2009, October 20), followed by a period;

- The subject line of the message with only the first letter of the first word in capitals. Follow the subject with a description of the posting in brackets [Web log message], [Online forum comment], [Electronic mailing list message], [Video file];
- "Retrieved from" with the URL where the message can be retrieved;
- If there is an address for an archived version of the message, include that address.

Database

Statistics Canada. (n.d.). *Crimes by type of offence.*

Retrieved from http://cansim2.statcan.ca

21-d APA-Style Sample Essay

The three main components of an APA essay are the title page, the text or body of the essay, and the list of references. The title page is page 1; it should include the following elements:

- the words *Running head:* and a short version of the paper's main title in the upper-left corner;
- the page number (1) in the upper-right corner;
- the full title of the essay, centred;
- identifying information (for a student paper, author's name, course name and section number, instructor's name, and date), centred.

Your essay may also include one or more appendixes. Appendixes follow the reference list and footnotes, if any, with each appendix beginning on a separate page.

On the following pages are excerpts from an APA-style essay.[2] Format specifications are pointed out in the marginal notes.

---

[2] Adapted from an essay by Kathleen Lenaghan, a student in a Sociology class.

Running head: DISCUSSING *QUIET RAGE*   1 ← Page number in upper right corner

Running head (first two
or three words of title
is identified) in upper
left-hand corner

Full title,
author's
name, course
name and
section
number,
instructor's
name, and
date centred
on page

Discussing *Quiet Rage: The Stanford Prison*

Experiment in

Sociological Terms

Kathleen Lenaghan

Sociology 1125, Section L16

Professor Ogden

April 10, 2008

Note: This sample title page includes the
course name and number, the date, and the
instructor's name. Check with your
instructor as to whether you should include
this information on your title page.

Philip Zimbardo conducted The Stanford Prison Experiment in 1971 to test the validity of his "dispositional hypothesis." The experiment that followed has become one of the most controversial sociological studies ever performed and one of the most referenced studies in sociology classrooms. This essay uses the sociological imagination to describe *Quiet Rage: The Stanford Prison Experiment* (1992), the film documenting the study, by relating the concepts of personal troubles to public issues. Additionally, this essay will discuss research methodology and ethics, concepts of statuses and roles, and the Thomas Theorem.

Background Information

Paragraphs indented five spaces → Zimbardo proposed, in the dispositional hypothesis, that people who seek careers as corrections officers are predisposed to the sadistic intimidation and degradation tactics seen in penitentiaries and thus enjoy work that allows them to express these tendencies, contrary to the generally accepted idea that guards become "hardened" after exposure to inmates over time. Zimbardo further asserted that prisoners were imprisoned because they lacked the ability to function in normal society. Therefore, the negative and violent conditions of prison are a result of the dispositions of the guards and inmates. To test this hypothesis, Zimbardo created a prison setting where "normal" people filled the roles of both prisoners and guards. He recruited 24 volunteers and randomly assigned them the role of guard or prisoner. To make the experiment realistic, police removed the prisoners from their homes and charged them with a false offence. After the police had fingerprinted and booked the prisoners, the guards blindfolded and transported the prisoners to the prison that had been set up in the basement of a building on campus. The initial timeline for the experiment was two weeks, but, as the behaviour of the guards became increasingly aggressive and the mental state of the prisoners deteriorated, Zimbardo halted the study after just six days. This experiment is both one of the most studied sociological experiments and one of the most controversial, due to the extreme behaviours of the participants and the debate over the ethics of the research method.

An important part of Zimbardo's research is the aspect of authority. The lengths that the guards were willing to go to in order to terrorize the prisoners were shocking, but, ultimately, they were following Zimbardo's instructions. One guard, "John Wayne," asserted that he took it as far as possible in order to perform his own experiment on the prisoners, but the vast majority of guards believed they were simply doing what Zimbardo wanted them to do. Stanley Milgram explored this trust in authority in his 1960 study where he found Americans to be "an obedient people: not blindly obedient, not blissfully obedient, just obedient" (Meyer, 1970, p. 58).

DISCUSSING *QUIET RAGE*   4

Research Method: Was It Ethical?

In evaluating the ethics of the Stanford Prison Experiment, a relevant set of standards is the 1949 Nuremberg Code (National Institutes of Health, 1949). The experiment adheres to the majority of the 10 requirements of the code, but deviates in some important areas. The participants in the study were voluntary and informed participants, which is the cornerstone of ethical research in experiments such as this one. Zimbardo designed the experiment to prove something that would benefit society; by using the findings of the study, he theorized that it would be possible to create prisons that were not so prone to violence.

Zimbardo breached the Nuremburg Code by refusing to allow Prisoner 8126 to leave. According to the Code, "the human subject should be at liberty to bring the research to an end if he has reached the physical or mental state when continuation of the research seems to him to be impossible" (McIntyre, 2006, p. 52).

The Sociological Imagination

According to C. Wright Mills in *The Sociological Imagination* (1959), the sociological imagination is "a quality of mind that will help [sociologists] to use information and to develop reason in order to achieve lucid summations of what is going on in the world and of what may be happening within themselves" (p. 5). He goes on to outline the three questions to ask when using the sociological imagination to evaluate a society: "What is the structure of this particular society as a whole? Where does this society stand in human history? What varieties of men and women… prevail in this society" (pp. 6–7)? These sociological questions can be applied to *Quiet Rage* as a means of understanding the behaviours of the prisoners and guards.

The social structure within the prison system was set up with the prisoners at the bottom of the hierarchy, with the guards holding authority over them. Above the guards was Zimbardo, who identified himself as the prison warden. This social structure is different from a "normal" social structure, where the interactions between the classes are dictated by social norms and folkways, because there are concrete rules that define the relationships between guards and prisoners. *The status quo* is maintained by regulating the behaviour of the prisoners and empowering the guards to exert their authority and control over them.

When examining where the prison society in *Quiet Rage* stands historically, it is important to recognize that the environment is artificial and its intended period of existence was only two weeks. Its historical significance comes from the information drawn from the study, rather than any growth and change that occurred within the prison society.

Ultimately, the person who prevailed in this constructed society was Zimbardo, who placed himself at the top of the social hierarchy. The guards also prevailed because Zimbardo gave them the power and authority to run the prison. This was appropriate as it mirrored the structure of real prisons in that period with white men generally in power.

Social Status, Roles, and Stigma

Status, role, and stigma are essential concepts for understanding the social relationships and identities of the participants in the Zimbardo study. A status is a social position held by a person within a society. In the Stanford Prison Experiment, Zimbardo divided the group into three statuses: the prisoners, the guards, and the warden. Zimbardo appointed himself as warden and then arbitrarily assigned statuses to student participants. The new statuses of "guard" or "prisoner" are the ascribed statuses of the participants. An important part of the prisoners' transition from their civilian status to their prisoner status was the degradation ceremony where they were stripped naked, hosed down, and then dressed in their uniforms. This helped to detach the prisoners from their pre-prison identity in order for them to accept their new status fully. This was an important process for the guards to go through as well because it reinforced their authority over the inmates, which was crucial for the social stratification within the prison setting. After a few days, the prisoners began to demonstrate their total internalization of their new roles by referring to themselves by their assigned numbers rather than their names. At this point in the study, prisoner status had replaced the individual pre-prison status as their master status. This kind of identity shift is evident in real prisoners as they replace their pre-prison self-image with a prison identity (Schmid & Jones, 1991).

References typed, centred, at top of page ⟶

References

Dyer, G. (2006). Anybody's son will do. In L. J. McIntyre (Ed.), *The practical skeptic: Readings in Sociology* (pp. 212–223). New York, NY: McGraw Hill.

Goffman, E. (2006). Presentation of self in everyday life. In L. J. McIntyre (Ed.), *The practical skeptic: Readings in Sociology* (pp. 58–68). New York, NY: McGraw Hill.

Hanging indent for reference entries ⟶

McIntyre, L. J. (2006) Doing the right thing: Ethics in research. In L. J. McIntyre (Ed.), *The practical skeptic: Readings in Sociology* (pp. 48–57). New York, NY: McGraw Hill.

Meyer, P. (1970, February). If Hitler asked you to execute a stranger, would you? Probably. *Esquire*, 72–73, 74, 128–132.

Mills, C. W. (1959). *The sociological imagination*. Oxford, United Kingdom: Oxford University Press.

National Institute of Health. (1949). Nuremberg code. Retrieved from http://ohsr.od.nih.gov /guidelines/nuremberg.html

Schmid, T. J., & Jones, R. S. (2006). Suspended identity: Identity transformation in a maximum security prison. In L. J. McIntyre (Ed.), *The practical skeptic: Readings in Sociology* (pp. 224–235). New York, NY: McGraw Hill.

Zimbardo, Philip G. (Director). (1992). *Quiet rage: The Stanford prison experiment* [DVD]. United States: Stanford University.

Note: APA style requires you to distinguish among different audio and video media. After the title of the work, indicate the medium of the work by using brackets: [Motion picture], [DVD], [Audio podcast], [Television series episode], [Demographic map], [record], [cassette], [CD]. With such a medium as a CD, APA asks that your in-text citation include the side, band, or track number. Thus, a reference to Stan Rogers's "Northwest Passage" would be cited as (Rogers, 1981, track 1).

Chicago style or CM (for Chicago Manual) style uses the same basic approach as MLA. The only complicated element in the Chicago formula is that there are two citation styles recommended in *The Chicago Manual of Style,* one that reflects APA practice and one that reflects the original MLA approach. The first uses the author–date system, while the second, the "humanities" version, uses superscript numbers in the body of the essay with a set of notes, either at the bottom of the page (footnotes) or on a separate page (endnotes) preceding the bibliography. We will focus on this number–note system.

There is one other variant: Chicago style distinguishes a block or extended quotation from an integrated, short quotation, which Chicago calls a "run-in" quotation, on the basis of length. Use block format for quotations longer than one hundred words or six to eight lines of text. As well, Chicago recommends using a block format when quoting two or more paragraphs, or any material requiring special formatting (e.g., lines of poetry, quotations next to one another for comparison). Present a block quotation by

- separating the quotation from your text by indenting it one tab;
- not using quotation marks to segregate it from your own text;
- adding the appropriate superscript number after the period that concludes your block quotation to signal the location of your endnote on the quotation's source.

22-a The Citation

Here is an example of a Chicago citation:

> If "blockbuster[s]: films that shatter the barrier between market segments"[1] is the appropriate category for the *Lord of the Rings* trilogy, it is clear that the mix of the fantasy, moral quest, and action genres accomplished in these films appeals to a wide range of market segments.*

If you were using the author–date system of Chicago style, you would insert (O'Brien and Szeman 2004) after "market segments."

The humanities format is different. Note that there is a superscript (raised) number following the quotation marks

---

*Extracted from Susie O'Brien and Imre Szeman, *Popular Culture: A User's Guide* (Toronto: Thomson Nelson, 2004), p. 120

that complete the quote. For an indirect borrowing, the note number could follow the period that concludes the sentence in which the borrowing appears. In Chicago style, you have a choice of placing the note either at the foot of the page on which the citation is made or on a separate page immediately preceding the bibliography page. We recommend you use the "endnotes" model because of its simplicity.

In the case above, your endnote would be

> 1. Susie O'Brien and Imre Szeman, *Popular Culture: A User's Guide* (Toronto: Thomson Nelson, 2004), 120.

Please note the following features of the number–note system recommended by *The Chicago Manual of Style* for humanities disciplines:

1. The numbering of the notes is cumulative.
2. The notes page is set up by centring the title, *Notes,* on the page, followed by consecutively numbered notes conveying the essential information for the sources of your citations.
3. Present the endnotes in a double spaced format, the same format Chicago style recommends for your whole paper.
4. Each note is indented three spaces for its first line and left-aligned for any other lines.
5. A second or subsequent note to a particular source should be done in a shortened form; for instance: 3. O'Brien and Szeman, *Popular Culture,* 33.

22-b The Bibliography

Chicago style for the humanities stipulates that the list of sources consulted for a paper should be called the bibliography. Please note the double-spacing of all examples here; you should also carefully observe the ways in which a note and a bibliography entry differ in format and use of internal punctuation.

For a complete listing, consult *The Chicago Manual of Style* in the reference section of your library or go to the following website: www.chicagomanualofstyle.org/home.html.

On this site, you can also view the Q&A section on the *Chicago Manual*, or sign up for a free trial of the *Manual* online site.

BOOKS

The bolded entries indicate the most commonly included elements:

- **author/editor/translator/institutional author, with full name in standard order for notes and surname first for bibliographic entries**
- **title, including subtitle**
- editor, translator, compiler, if one appears on the title page
- edition, if the second or subsequent edition
- volume, if applicable
- series title, if applicable
- **facts of publication—city, publisher, date of publication**
- page number(s), if the reference is to part of a larger whole
- URL and other information for online books

In each of the following examples, "NOTE" stands for the format to be used in a footnote or endnote, and "BIBLIO" stands for the format required in a bibliographic entry.

Book by one author

NOTE

1. Kay J. Anderson, *Vancouver's Chinatown: Racial Discourse in Canada, 1875–1980* (Montreal: McGill-Queen's University Press, 1995), 34.

BIBLIO

Anderson, Kay J. *Vancouver's Chinatown: Racial Discourse in Canada, 1875–1980*. Montreal: McGill-Queen's University Press, 1995.

Two or more works by the same author In a bibliography, if you have two or more works by the same author, use a 3-em dash in place of the author's name for the second and subsequent entries.

BIBLIO

Murakami, Haruki. *IQ84*. Translated by Jay Rubin and Philip Gabriel. Toronto: Bond Street, 2011.

———. *The Wind-Up Bird Chronicle*. Translated by Jay Rubin. Toronto: Borzoi, 1997.

Translations and publishers imprints The above examples also illustrate how to present translators' names in a bibliography entry and how to deal with publishers' imprints. The *Chicago Manual* suggests that, as imprints change hands, you omit the publisher's name and only include the imprint name. The exception to this is when you are faced with a joint imprint or some other kind of ambiguity. In such cases, you present both names with a space and a slash between each name (Smith/Thomas).

Book by two or three authors or editors Start entries with the authors' or editors' names in full.

NOTE: John Frederick Nims and David Mason,

BIBLIO: Nims, John Frederick, and David Mason.

Book by more than three authors

NOTE: James Reinking et al.,

BIBLIO: Reinking, James, Andrew Hart, Robert van der Osten, Sue Ann Cairns, and Robert Fleming.

Book with a corporate or institutional author

NOTE

2. American Psychological Association, *Publication Manual of the American Psychological Association,* 5th ed. (Washington, DC: American Psychological Association, 2001), 105.

BIBLIO

American Psychological Association. *Publication Manual of the American Psychological Association.* 5th ed. Washington, DC: American Psychological Association, 2001.

Selection from an anthology or similar collection   In a bibliography entry, give the full page range for the entire poem, story, essay, or chapter you're citing from the anthology. (Here, Layton's poem is less than one page.)

NOTE

3. Irving Layton, "The Way the World Ends," in *The Norton Introduction to Literature,* 6th ed., ed. Carl Bain, Jerome Beaty, and J. Paul Hunter (New York: W. W. Norton, 1995), 833.

BIBLIO

Layton, Irving. "The Way the World Ends." In *The Norton Introduction to Literature,* 6th ed., edited by Carl Bain, Jerome Beaty, and J. Paul Hunter, 833. New York: W. W. Norton, 1995.

Anthology or edited book

NOTE

4. R. S. Gwynn, ed., *Literature: A Pocket Anthology* (Toronto: Addison-Wesley Educational Publishers, 2002).

BIBLIO

Gwynn, R. S., ed. *Literature: A Pocket Anthology.* Toronto: Addison-Wesley Educational Publishers, 2002.

Government publication   Format a note and a bibliographic entry for a publication by a government department or agency in the same way you would for a corporate author. The name of the government department or agency responsible for the publication becomes the author entry and the name of the publication is the title. In recording the publication data, look first for the city of publication and second for the government printer. Finally, record the year of publication, and, for the note form only, the page reference for your quotation or borrowing.

PERIODICALS

The Chicago Manual of Style uses the term *periodical* for scholarly and professional journals, magazines, and newspapers. The elements to be included are

- author's or authors' names;
- title and subtitle of article or column;
- title of periodical, magazine, or newspaper;
- issue information (volume, issue number, date);
- page reference (use a single page reference for a direct reference to a sentence or paragraph and an inclusive page reference for a general reference to an article).

Journals

NOTE

5. Lorraine York, "Letters in Canada 2002: Fiction," *University of Toronto Quarterly* 23, no. 1 (2003–4): 5–6.

BIBLIO

York, Lorraine. "Letters in Canada 2002: Fiction." *University of Toronto Quarterly* 23, no. 1 (2003–4): 4–14.

The Chicago Manual of Style states that the issue number does not need to be given for journals that use continuous pagination throughout the year or for journals that list the month or season before the year.

Article from a monthly magazine For magazine citations, you may cite either a specific page number, or, if you are referring to the whole article, the range of page numbers for the article.

NOTE

12. John Douglas Belshaw, "The Lost Plague: Why We Have Forgotten One of Canada's Most Devastating Smallpox Epidemics," *Walrus*, May 2013, 20.

BIBLIO

Belshaw, John Douglas. "The Lost Plague: Why We Have Forgotten One of Canada's Most Devastating Smallpox Epidemics." *Walrus*, May 2013, 19–20.

Article from a weekly magazine

NOTE

6. Jonathon Gatehouse, "When Science Goes Silent," *Maclean's*, May 13, 2013, 18.

BIBLIO

Gatehouse, Jonathon. "When Science Goes Silent." *Maclean's*, May 13, 2013, 16–20.

Unsigned article from a weekly or monthly magazine

NOTE

8. "Get Fit? Get Real," *Consumer Reports*, February 2009, 31.

BIBLIO

Consumer Reports. "Get Fit? Get Real." February 2009, 30–32.

The bibliographic entry is written the same as the note but without a number and with a period after the article title instead of a comma.

Signed article from a daily newspaper   Chicago style notes that, in different editions of a daily newspaper, page numbers vary, so omit the page number but include the edition (final edition) or the section (sec. B) the article is in.

> **NOTE**
>
> 6. Cheryl Chan, "Arrest in Russia Shocks Author of Gay Fairy Tale," *Province*, May 8, 2013, sec. A.
>
> **BIBLIO**
>
> Chan, Cheryl. "Arrest in Russia Shocks Author of Gay Fairy Tale." *Province*, May 8, 2013, sec. A.

Unsigned article from a daily newspaper Basically, you write the note for an unsigned article in a newspaper the same way as for a signed article. The one adjustment you have to make is to move the article's title into the place normally reserved for the author's name.

You would write the bibliographic note with the name of the newspaper where the author's name would normally appear.

ELECTRONIC SOURCES

In its comments on electronic sources, *The Chicago Manual of Style* initially stresses the fact that electronic texts are subject to change in a way that printed texts are not—changes in address and changes in content. Electronic articles are also not necessarily subject to the review by publishers and peers that is part of academic publishing in other media. As such, the *Manual* stresses that writers must take special pains to ensure their borrowing is current, accurate, and accessible.

In citing an electronic source, writers are asked to add two elements not present in the citation of a printed text: in some cases, the date the source was accessed; and the locating information such as a DOI (digital object identifier) or URL (web address). Aside from these two additional elements, the citation takes the same format recommended for a printed text, whether a book, an article, or another genre.

Simply add to the entry these two concluding elements:

- If your discipline requires it, the date (month, day, year) you accessed the material. Otherwise, access dates are not required for citations of formally published electronic sources. For less formal publications (blogs, wikis, web pages), you should include the date that the information was last modified, or, failing that, give the access date, as less formal publications are not stable and could change over time.
- The DOI of your source (if available), or the URL

For example, for an article in an online encyclopedia, you would give the information for an encyclopedia entry, and then add the two elements required for electronic sources:

NOTE

1. *Wikipedia*, s.v. "Canadian Literary Magazines," last modified February. 14, 2013, http://en.wikipedia.org/wiki/Category:Canadian _literary_magazines.

BIBLIO

Wikipedia. Wikimedia Foundation, Inc. Accessed February 23, 2013. http://en.wikipedia.org /wiki/Main_Page.

Besides these two main guidelines, URLs, DOIs, and email addresses can be broken where there is a slash, double slash, period, colon, an equals sign, an ampersand, or other punctuation or symbols.

BOOKS AND EBOOKS

The *Chicago Manual* was the first style guide to recognize that people might be using an electronic edition of a text they are citing. Chicago notes that in citing such a text, you should simply add to the end of the entry the format the book is in: Kindle edition, PDF ebook, Microsoft Reader ebook, Palm eBook, or EPUB (common in public libraries). The one difference in the note for such a reference is that, as Chicago suggests, page numbers may not be stable, so it is better to cite the chapter or section of the book that your reference is from.

NOTE

5. Douglas J. Preston, *The Monster of Florence*, (New York: Grand Central, 2008), EPUB, ch 5.

BIBLIO

Preston, Douglas J. *The Monster of Florence*. New York: Grand Central, 2008. EPUB.

Electronic versions of books

As well as ebooks, you will read electronic versions of books online. This is particularly common with books that are no longer under copyright and are in the public domain. Before the advent of electronic archives, such texts could be very hard to find and access. Sites such as Project Gutenberg are a godsend to someone researching older works. When citing such books, be guided by Chicago's standard note and bibliography format for books (when the information is provided by the website) and add the DOI, if it is available, or the URL. You may also find different file formats for books found online (e.g., HTML, EPUB, or a plain text file). Make note of the format at the end of your bibliography entry or before the chapter or section number in a note. Ebooks online may also include the date they were uploaded to the Web rather than conventional publication information. Ask your instructor if you should include this information. At present, Chicago is silent on this and some other variants you may run into.

NOTE

12. Nellie McClung, *Clearing in the West: My Own Story,* (1935; Project Gutenberg, 2011), EPUB, chap. 8, http://gutenberg.ca/ebooks/mcclung -clearinginthewest/mcclung-clearinginthewest-00 -h-dir/mcclung-clearinginthewest-00-h.html.

13. Herman Melville, *Moby Dick,* http: //www.literaturepage.com/read/mobydick-1 .html, chap. 24.

BIBLIO

McClung, Nellie. *Clearing in the West: My Own Story.* Reprint of the 1935 Toronto edition, Project Gutenberg, 2011. EPUB.

Woolf, Virginia. *To the Lighthouse.* Accessed 11 August 2013. http://www.bookmate.com /r#d=GkMjnwY7.

PERIODICALS

The same general guideline applies to articles in periodicals. Simply give the usual list of identifying details, including the page reference if available, and add the DOI or URL. Where there are no page numbers, use another locator such as a subheading. The examples below illustrate the citations for four different kinds of periodicals. Only the note format is included here because the differences between note and bibliography format are slight, and you should be familiar with them by this point.

Journal article, published conventionally, with a DOI
Access date is only included if required by your instructor or discipline; in general, Chicago style does not include the date of access for electronic journal articles.

NOTE

1. Benjamin G. Van Allen and Volker H. W. Rudolf, "Ghosts of Habitats Past: Environmental Carry-Over Effects Drive Population Dynamics in Novel Habitat," *American Naturalist* 181, no. 5 (2013): 601, accessed May 15, 2013, doi:10.1086/670127.

BIBLIO

Van Allen, Benjamin G. and Volker H. W. Rudolf. "Ghosts of Habitats Past: Environmental Carry-Over Effects Drive Population Dynamics in Novel Habitat." *American Naturalist* 181, no. 5 (2013): 596–608. Accessed May 15, 2013. doi: 10. 1086/670127.

If your journal article gives both an issue number and a month of publication, you need not include the month of publication with the year in parentheses. However, if there is a volume number and no issue number, include the month of publication if it is given. Where there is no DOI, give the URL (a stable URL is provided by most online databases and archives of academic materials, such as JSTOR).

Journal article published in online format only   The journal below is an exception in that it does not use volume and issue numbers, but only date; if volume and issue are available, they must be included.

NOTE

11. Marina L. Levitina, "Models of New Femininity and Masculinity in Soviet Russia in the 1920s," *Kinema: A Journal for Film and Audiovisual Media*, Spring 2013, http://www.kinema.uwaterloo.ca/issue.php?year=2013&season=1.

BIBLIO

Levitina, Marina L. "Models of New Femininity and Masculinity in Soviet Russia in the 1920s." *Kinema: A Journal for Film and Audiovisual Media*, Spring 2013, http://www.kinema.uwaterloo.ca/issue.php?year=2013&season=1.

Article published in a magazine in both conventional and online formats
If you have consulted an article online, make sure you include the DOI, if available, or the URL for the article.

NOTE

    1. Jonathon Gatehouse, "When Science Goes Silent," *Maclean's*, May 3, 2013, http://www2 .macleans.ca/2013/05/03/when-science-goes -silent/.

Article in an online newspaper

NOTE

    15. Meredith Bennett-Smith, "Brazilian 'Atlantis': Submersible Finds Possible Evidence of Continent Deep beneath Atlantic Ocean," *Huffington Post*, May 7, 2013, http: //www.huffingtonpost.com/2013 /05/07 /brazilian-atlantis-japanese-submersible -atlantic-ocean_n_3231437.html?ir=World.

LINE BREAKS IN URLS AND DOIS

Section 14.2 of *The Chicago Manual of Style* notes that necessary line breaks in URLs and DOIs should occur after a colon (:) or double slash (//); but before a single slash (/), a tilde (~), a period (.), a comma (,), a hyphen (-), an underline (_), a question mark (?), a number sign (#) or a percent symbol (%); and either before or after an equal sign (=) or an ampersand (&).

Basic Grammar

Words can be divided into nine parts of speech: noun, pronoun, verb, adjective, adverb, conjunction, preposition, article, and interjection.

23-a Nouns

Nouns are words that name persons, places, things, or ideas.

> *Trudeau* remained a mysterious and reclusive *figure* for many *Canadians.*

From these examples and others you can study for yourself, certain properties of the noun should become clear.

1. Nouns are frequently preceded by words like *the, a, an, my, your, some, each, every, his, this,* and *that.*

2. The most traditional positions for nouns are before the verb, after the verb, and after a preposition.

3. Nouns may be singular or plural in number. The plural form of a noun is most frequently formed by adding *-s* or *-es* to the singular form. Some nouns have only one form for both the singular and the plural (*moose, moose*). Other nouns are irregular in the way the singular form differs from the plural form (*wife, wives*).

4. Nouns tend to have certain endings that distinguish them from verbs or adjectives: *-ness, -ism, -ance, -ment.*

5. Nouns may function as subjects or objects. In the sentence *Shelley took the book from the shelf,* the noun *Shelley* is the subject, the noun *book* is the object, and the noun *shelf* is the object of the preposition *from.*

6. The apostrophe is used to form the possessive case of nouns (*Simpson's* lawn). The possessive case of singular nouns, including those that end in *-s,* is formed by adding *-'s* (*needle's* point, *Jones's* boat). The possessive case of plural nouns that end in *-s* is formed by adding only an apostrophe (*needles'* points).

7. Nouns can be classified into four categories according to the kind of entity they represent: a *common* noun names a general entity *(car)*; a *proper* noun names a particular member of a class *(Chevrolet)*; an *abstract* noun names a quality or idea that is not tangible *(beauty)*; a *concrete* noun names something that is tangible *(grass)*. For more on proper nouns see 59-b.

8. A collective noun names a group of entities. Though it refers to more than one entity, its form is singular *(crowd, jury, team, committee)*. A singular pronoun is used to replace a collective noun (a *team* and *its* record) unless that noun refers to individual members of the group (a *team* and *their* paycheques).

ESL Focus | COUNTABLE AND NONCOUNTABLE NOUNS

There are two classes of nouns in English: countable and noncountable. Countable nouns name things that may be counted. They can be used with *one, a* or *an, the, many, several, some, few,* and numbers:

> five girls, the tree, several rocks, a few cities, many ideas

Singular countable nouns cannot appear alone. They must follow an article or a demonstrative or possessive adjective:

> a book, the pen, his ear, their project, this feeling, that rock

Plural countable nouns can appear alone, with *the,* or with numbers:

> teachers, the teachers, ten teachers

Noncountable nouns—which are sometimes called uncountable nouns or mass nouns—name things that are measured by their mass. They include some nouns that express abstraction:

> water, oxygen, butter, gold

> advice, anger, honesty, integrity

continued

Noncountable nouns cannot be used with the indefinite articles *a* and *an*.

~~a~~ water, ~~an~~ oxygen, ~~an~~ advice, ~~an~~ integrity

Noncountable nouns can be used with *some, any,* or *more* to express quantity. They can also be connected to a countable noun to specify an amount:

any water, ten litres of water, some honesty

Most noncountable nouns do not have a plural form:

advice, equipment, garbage, information, money, scenery

Nouns such as *candy, cereal, cheese, chicken, chocolate, fish, paper,* and *wine* can be countable or noncountable depending on their function in the sentence.

COUNT

I ate *two* candies. [countable pieces of candy]

NONCOUNT

I like to eat *candy*. [general food type]

23-b Pronouns

A **pronoun** is a word that takes the place of a noun. The noun that the pronoun replaces is known as the pronoun's *antecedent.*

Although the *country* is rich, *it* has high unemployment.

Pronouns fall into nine categories: personal, possessive, reflexive, intensive, demonstrative, relative, interrogative, indefinite, and reciprocal.

PERSONAL PRONOUNS

A personal pronoun refers to specific persons or things. Personal pronouns agree with their antecedents in number and gender, but their case depends on their function in a sentence. Table 24-1 lists the thirty case forms of the personal pronoun. For more information about pronoun case, see Chapter 41.

POSSESSIVE PRONOUNS

A possessive pronoun indicates ownership.

> John lost *his* wallet.

> The employees are preparing *their* response to the layoffs.

TABLE 23-1 Personal Pronouns

SINGULAR	SUBJECTIVE CASE	OBJECTIVE CASE	POSSESSIVE CASE
First person	I	me	my, mine
Second person	you	you	your, yours
Third person (masculine)	he	him	his
Third person (feminine)	she	her	her, hers
Third person (neuter)	it	it	its
PLURAL			
First person	we	us	our, ours
Second person	you	you	your, yours
Third person (all genders)	they	them	their, theirs

REFLEXIVE PRONOUNS

Reflexive pronouns, which refer back to the subject of the sentence or clause in which they appear, are used to denote an action where the recipient and the doer are the same person or thing. A reflexive pronoun is formed by adding *self* or *-selves* to a personal pronoun.

> Did you hurt *yourself*?

INTENSIVE PRONOUNS

Intensive pronouns are used to emphasize a noun (or its equivalent). They have the same form as reflexive pronouns.

> The voters spoke to the prime minister *himself*.

DEMONSTRATIVE PRONOUNS

A demonstrative pronoun identifies or points to a noun.

> *That* is my main objective.   *This* is our finest china.

RELATIVE PRONOUNS

A relative pronoun introduces an adjective clause (see 24-f) and refers back to the noun or pronoun that the clause modifies.

The candidate *who* won the debate lost the election.

Tomas found the keys *that* he had misplaced.

The relative pronouns *who*, *whose*, and *whom* refer to people; *which* refers to inanimate objects, animals, and groups of persons; and *that* refers to either things or persons. For more information about *that* and *which*, see 42-b.

INTERROGATIVE PRONOUNS

An interrogative pronoun introduces a question. Interrogative pronouns include *who*, *whom*, *whose*, *which*, and *what*.

Who scored the winning goal for Canada in the 2010 olympic gold medal hockey game?

Which book won the Giller Prize?

INDEFINITE PRONOUNS

An indefinite pronoun makes a reference to a non-specific person or thing. Indefinite pronouns include *all*, *another*, *any*, *anyone*, *anything*, *each*, *everybody*, *everyone*, *everything*, *few*, *many*, *nobody*, *none*, *one*, *several*, *some*, and *somebody*. Many of these words may function as either pronouns or adjectives.

Does *anyone* know the solution to the problem? [pronoun]

Each client must pay a service fee. [adjective]

RECIPROCAL PRONOUNS

A reciprocal pronoun expresses a mutual relationship. There are only two reciprocal pronouns: *one another* and *each other*.

The two men complimented *each other* on their ties.

23-c Verbs

A **verb** is a word that expresses an action or a state of being. All verbs except *be* have four principal parts.

BASE FORM	I *open* the door.
PAST TENSE	I *opened* the door.
PAST PARTICIPLE	I have *opened* the door.
PRESENT PARTICIPLE	I am *opening* the door.

See Table 23-2 for verb tenses.

TRANSITIVE AND INTRANSITIVE VERBS

A *transitive* verb takes an object, while an *intransitive* verb does not. An object is needed to complete the meaning of a transitive verb.

TABLE 23-2   Verb Tenses

PRESENT TENSE	
SIMPLE PRESENT	The simple present indicates actions or conditions that are occurring now.
I stand you stand he, she, it stands	we stand you stand they stand
PRESENT PROGRESSIVE	The present progressive indicates actions or conditions that are ongoing.
I am standing you are standing he, she, it is standing	we are standing you are standing they are standing
PRESENT PERFECT	The present perfect indicates actions or conditions that began in the past and continue into the present.
I have stood you have stood he, she, it has stood	we have stood you have stood they have stood
PRESENT PERFECT PROGRESSIVE	The present perfect progressive indicates actions or conditions that began in the past, continue into the present, and may extend into the future.
I have been standing you have been standing he, she, it has been standing	we have been standing you have been standing they have been standing

continued

TABLE 23-2 Verb Tenses (continued)

PAST TENSE

SIMPLE PAST

The simple past indicates actions or conditions that occurred in the past.

I stood	we stood
you stood	you stood
he, she, it stood	they stood

PAST PROGRESSIVE

The past progressive indicates ongoing actions or conditions that occurred in the past.

I was standing	we were standing
you were standing	you were standing
he, she, it was standing	they were standing

PAST PERFECT

The past perfect indicates actions or conditions that occurred in the past and were completed before some other past actions or conditions occurred.

I had stood	we had stood
you had stood	you had stood
he, she, it had stood	they had stood

PAST PERFECT PROGRESSIVE

The past perfect progressive indicates ongoing actions or conditions in the past that began before some other past actions or conditions began.

I had been standing	we had been standing
you had been standing	you had been standing
he, she, it had been standing	they had been standing

FUTURE TENSE

SIMPLE FUTURE

The simple future indicates actions or conditions that have yet to occur.

I will stand	we will stand
you will stand	you will stand
he, she, it will stand	they will stand

FUTURE PROGRESSIVE

The future progressive indicates ongoing actions or conditions that will occur in the future.

I will be standing	we will be standing
you will be standing	you will be standing
he, she, it will be standing	they will be standing

TABLE 23-2 Verb Tenses (continued)

FUTURE PERFECT	The future perfect indicates actions or conditions that will be completed by some definite time in the future.
I will have stood you will have stood she, it will have stood	we will have stood you will have stood they will have stood
FUTURE PERFECT PROGRESSIVE	The future perfect progressive indicates ongoing actions or conditions that will be completed by some definite time in the future.
I will have been standing you will have been standing he, she, it will have been standing	we will have been standing you will have been standing they will have been standing

TRANSITIVE   The Harper government accumulated the largest deficit in Canadian history. [The object *deficit* completes the meaning of the verb.]

INTRANSITIVE   The hockey players gathered at centre ice [The verb has no receiver.]

LINKING VERBS

A linking verb (V) connects the subject (S) with a *subject complement* (SC), a word or word group that identifies or describes the subject.

```
 ┌──S──┐ ┌─V─┐ ┌───────────SC──────
The economy remains the most important campaign
 ─────
issue.
```

The most common linking verbs are *appear, become, feel, look, remain, seem, smell, sound, taste,* and forms of *be*.

ESL Focus   HELPING VERBS

Helping verbs (also known as *auxiliary* verbs) combine with main verbs to indicate tense. The most common helping verbs are forms of *be, have,* and *do*.

continued

The forms of be (am, is, are, was, were, and will be) combine with the present-participle form of a verb (the -ing form) to create the progressive tense (see Table 23-2). The tense of the helping verb determines whether the past, present, or future progressive tense is formed.

I *am* writing a letter to confirm our agreement.

I *was* writing the letter when the phone call interrupted me.

The past-tense form of be combines with the past-participle form of a verb (the form ending in -d, -ed, -n, -en, or -t) to create the passive voice (see Chapter 46).

The letter *was* not *written* because of that interruption.

The forms of *do* are used to establish questions, emphasis, and negation.

QUESTION	*Do* you want to finish the letter?
EMPHASIS	I *did* want to finish that letter.
NEGATION	I *don't* know when I will finish the letter.

NOTE: For questions, use forms of *do* when forms of be are not part of the answer. (*Do* you know what he said? Yes, I *do*.) Use forms of be when forms of that verb are part of the answer. (*Are* you going to the party? Yes, I *am*.)

The forms of *have* combine with the past-participle form to create the perfect tense.

PRESENT PERFECT	I *have* finished the letter confirming our agreement.
PAST PERFECT	I *had* finished the letter before you arrived.
FUTURE PERFECT	I *will have* finished the letter before you arrive.

Modal auxiliaries are helping verbs that express obligation, necessity, probability, and ability. Unlike

continued

the forms of *be, have,* and *do,* modals do not change form to indicate tense. There are nine modals: *can, could, will, would, may, might, must, shall,* and *should.*

OBLIGATION	My brother *should* wash the car.
NECESSITY	My brother *must* wash the car.
PROBABILITY	My brother *may* wash the car.
ABILITY	My brother *can* wash the car.

IRREGULAR VERBS

Although most verbs in English follow a regular pattern, there are some two hundred irregular verbs. To learn how irregular verbs are conjugated, consult a dictionary.

VERBALS

A verbal is a verb form that does not function as a verb in a sentence. There are three kinds of verbals: infinitives, participles, and gerunds. *Infinitives* can function as nouns, adjectives, or adverbs.

NOUN	*To win* is gratifying.
ADJECTIVE	They had little opportunity *to respond.*
ADVERB	He waited *to see* the replay.

Participles, whether present or past, function as adjectives.

PRESENT PARTICIPLE	The *speeding* car was pulled over by the police.
PAST PARTICIPLE	The job required a *skilled* carpenter.

Gerunds have the same form as present participles, but they function in sentences as nouns.

GERUND	*Eating* is a necessity of life.

ESL Focus — GERUNDS AND INFINITIVES AFTER VERBS

A gerund is a verbal ending in *-ing (running, creating)*. An infinitive is a verbal consisting of the base form of a verb preceded by *to (to run, to create)*. Gerunds and infinitives that follow verbs function as direct objects (words or word groups that name the person or thing acted upon by the subject).

GERUND AS OBJECT	He enjoyed *winning* the race.
INFINITIVE AS OBJECT	She agreed *to run* for office.

Whether a gerund or an infinitive functions as the object in a sentence depends on the verb. Some verbs can be followed by a gerund but not by an infinitive. Other verbs can be followed by an infinitive but not by a gerund. Still other verbs can be followed by either a gerund or an infinitive.

VERBS FOLLOWED BY GERUND ONLY

admit	discuss	keep	recall
appreciate	enjoy	miss	regret
avoid	escape	postpone	risk
consider	finish	practise	stop
deny	imagine	quit	spend

• I regretted *spending* the money.

VERBS FOLLOWED BY INFINITIVE ONLY

agree	expect	mean	promise
ask	have	need	refuse
beg	hope	offer	wait
claim	intend	plan	want
decide	manage	pretend	wish

• They need to *lower* their expectations.

continued

VERBS FOLLOWED BY EITHER GERUND OR INFINITIVE

begin	hate	love	start
continue	like	prefer	try

- We began *counting* the votes. [gerund]

- We began to *count* the votes. [infinitive]

VOICE

The voice of a verb depends on whether the grammatical subject of the verb *acts* or *is acted upon*. If the subject acts, the verb is in the *active voice;* if it is acted upon, the verb is in the *passive voice.*

ACTIVE VOICE	The quarterback *threw* the ball downfield. [The quarterback *acts.*]
PASSIVE VOICE	The ball *was thrown* downfield by the quarterback. [The ball is *acted upon.*]

CHANGING PASSIVE VOICE INTO ACTIVE VOICE

1. *Transitive verbs and passive voice:*

Some passive structures use a transitive verb (an action verb), which takes an object. In these sentences, the receiver of the action is the subject of the sentence, and the doer of the action is the object of the preposition *by.*

Passive voice

```
                      ┌object of┐
    ┌ S ┐┌── V ──┐│ prep by │
```
That music was composed by Mozart.

To change this structure into active voice, give the sentence a subject that commits the action.

Active voice

```
   ┌─S─┐┌─V─┐ ┌ DO ┐
```
Mozart composed that music.

2. *Passive structures that do not name anything that commits the action:*

In some passive structures, we are not told who or what is doing the action.

Passive voice

```
 ┌S┐ ┌──V──┐ ┌──────────DO──────────
It was suggested that students buy a good Canadian
dictionary.
```

To turn this kind of passive structure into active voice, you need to supply the sentence with a subject committing the action.

Active voice

```
 ┌───S───┐┌─V─┐┌────────DO────────
Instructors suggest that students buy a good
Canadian dictionary.
```

MOOD

Verbs may be cast in different moods depending on whether the writer wishes to make a factual statement *(indicative mood)*, give a command *(imperative mood),* or express possibility rather than actuality *(subjunctive mood)*. Generally, writers do not have difficulty distinguishing between the indicative and the imperative moods.

INDICATIVE   Toronto is in many respects the Chicago of Canada. [statement]

IMPERATIVE   Get me the evening newspaper. [command]

The subjunctive mood is more challenging. In the present subjunctive, the base form of the verb is used.

SUBJUNCTIVE   They proposed that she ˄ ~~leaves~~ *leave* as soon as possible.

SUBJUNCTIVE   It is essential that you ˄ ~~are~~ *be* appointed to the committee.

In the past subjunctive, the form of *be* is *were*.

SUBJUNCTIVE If I ~~was~~ *were* you, I'd follow his advice.

FORMS OF THE SUBJUNCTIVE

Formal writing requires the use of the subjunctive mood in statements about hypothetical conditions; *that* clauses following verbs that request, order, or recommend; and dependent clauses (see 24-f) beginning with *as if* or *as though*.

Hypothetical conditions The subjunctive mood is used to express a condition that is wished for or imagined.

If I ~~was~~ *were* wealthy, I would quit this stupid job.

That clauses The subjunctive mood is used in *that* clauses following verbs such as *ask, command, insist, order, request, recommend,* and *suggest.*

The lawyers ask that the verdict ~~is~~ *be* overturned.

As if, as though *clauses* The subjunctive is used in *as if* and *as though* clauses, which express a hypothetical comparison.

The rookie politician delivered his speech as if he ~~was~~ *were* a contestant in a speed-skating contest.

23-d Adjectives and Adverbs

Adjectives and adverbs are words used to modify other words. **Adjectives** are easier to understand than adverbs, since they modify only nouns or pronouns.

The *confident* investor purchased *one thousand* shares. [modify the nouns *investor* and *shares*]

Adverbs modify verbs (or verbals), adjectives, other adverbs, or even entire clauses. Whereas adjectives answer the questions *which? what kind?* and *how many?* adverbs specify *in what manner, where, when, why,* and *how much.*

We drove *slowly* around the block. [modifies the verb *drove*]

Antibiotics have proven to be an *extremely* important medical advance. [modifies the adjective *important*]

He plays the game *very* well. [modifies the adverb *well*]

Ironically, the spokesperson for Mothers Against Drunk Drivers was charged with impaired driving. [modifies the entire clause]

COMPARATIVES AND SUPERLATIVES

When comparing two items, use the comparative form of the appropriate adjectives and adverbs.

Chocolate is *better* than licorice.

When comparing more than two items, use the superlative form of the appropriate adjectives and adverbs.

Of all candy, chocolate is *best*.

The comparative of one-syllable and some two-syllable adjectives is formed by adding -*er* and the superlative, by adding -*est (large, larger, largest)*. The comparative of many adjectives of two or more syllables is formed by adding *more* and the superlative by adding *most (careful, more careful, most careful; interesting, more interesting, most interesting)*.

The comparative of adjectives ending in -*y* is formed by replacing the -*y* with -*ier*, and the superlative by replacing the -*y* with -*iest*. Do not form double comparatives or double superlatives by adding *more* or *most* to these forms of the comparative and superlative.

He was the *happiest* [not the *most happiest*] person there.

The following adjectives and adverbs have irregular comparative and superlative forms.

BASE FORM	COMPARATIVE	SUPERLATIVE
bad	worse	worst
badly	worse	worst
good	better	best
well	better	best
little	less	least
many	more	most
much	more	most
some	more	most

ESL Focus · INFINITIVES AND PARTICIPLES AS ADJECTIVES

In English, it is possible to use an infinitive or participle after certain verbs. When using *-ing* and *-ed* verbals as adjectives, be aware that your choice between the two endings will have a profound effect on the meaning of your statement.

The *exhausting* man made Manjinder uncomfortable. [The man was tiring to be with.]

The *exhausted* man made Manjinder uncomfortable. [The man was tired.]

CUMULATIVE AND COORDINATE ADJECTIVES

A series of adjectives can be cumulative or coordinate. A *cumulative* series is a sequence of adjectives in which each adjective modifies its successor *(light blue tweed material)*. Note that the adjectives in a cumulative series are not separated by commas.

In a *coordinate* series, the adjectives all modify the same noun and are therefore separated by commas *(talented, industrious, ambitious entrepreneurs)*. When coordinate adjectives are similar in nature, their order is unimportant *(smelly, overheated, humid room* and *overheated, smelly, humid room* are both acceptable). Order becomes an issue, however, when adjectives of different kinds occur in a series. You cannot say, for instance, *Norwegian, ten, fat, older gentlemen.* The following list will help you determine the correct order for your coordinate adjectives.

1. *Number or comparative or superlative form:* the, second, larger, smallest

2. *Evaluative adjective:* sour, dedicated, handsome

3. *Size:* huge, tiny, long

4. *Shape:* rectangular, round, ovoid

5. *Age:* old, young, eighteenth-century

6. *Colour:* magenta, green, scarlet

7. *Nationality:* Swedish, Canadian, Filipino

8. *Religion:* Muslim, Protestant, Jewish

9. *Material:* ceramic, pewter, wood

10. *Noun as adjective:* faculty lounge, student centre, economics curriculum

ESL Focus   PLACEMENT OF ADVERBS

The placement of adverbs can cause ESL writers difficulty. By mastering a few rules, however, you can overcome that difficulty.

1. The position of an adverb is determined by what kind of adverb it is.

   a. Adverbs of *manner* (how a task is done) appear in the middle or at the end of the sentence.

      I *quickly* bent my mind to the task.

      I bent my mind to the task *quickly.*

   b. Adverbs of *time* are placed at the beginning or end of the sentence.

      In the morning, I eat lightly.

   c. Adverbs of *place* appear at the end of the sentence.

      He opened the door and went *into the room.*

   d. Adverbs of *degree or emphasis* are placed directly in front of the word they modify.

      He is *almost* ready to go to the game.

   e. Adverbs of *frequency* are placed in the middle if they modify the verb and at the beginning if they modify the sentence.

      She *always* likes to play golf.

      Usually, she is early for her tee time.

continued

2. An adverb that modifies an adjective or another adverb is placed before the word it modifies.

> Tuition is *extremely* high today. [modifies the adjective *high*]

EXCEPTION: The adverb *enough* always follows the adjective or adverb it modifies.

> She dances well *enough*.

Do not place an adverb between a transitive verb and its direct object.

INCORRECT	He threw *quickly* the ball to the catcher.
REVISED	He *quickly* threw the ball to the catcher.

23-e Conjunctions

Conjunctions link words or word groups to one another and show the relationship between the elements connected.

COORDINATING CONJUNCTIONS

Coordinating conjunctions *(and, but, yet, or, for, nor, so)* join grammatically equal words, phrases, or clauses.

> Shirley *and* Joseph have never got past their initial dislike of each other. [joins the words *Shirley* and *Joseph*]

> You can park the scooter on the street *or* in the garage. [joins the phrases *on the street* and *in the garage*]

SUBORDINATING CONJUNCTIONS

Subordinating conjunctions introduce dependent, or subordinate, clauses (see 24-f) and show the relationship between those clauses and independent clauses (see 24-e).

Unless the economy slows down, signs of inflation are bound to appear.

Following is a list of common subordinating conjunctions:

after	even though	so that	when
although	if	than	whenever
as	in order that	that	where
as if	once	though	whereas
because	rather than	unless	wherever
before	since	until	while

CORRELATIVE CONJUNCTIONS

Correlative conjunctions are pairs of conjunctions that join equal words or word groups.

both/and	neither/nor	not only/but also
either/or	not/but	whether/or

The joined words or word groups should be parallel grammatical elements.

Either the newspaper prints a retraction *or* it faces a lawsuit.

For information about faulty parallel structure, see 39-d.

23-f Prepositions

Prepositions are connecting words that show the relationships between nouns or pronouns and other words in a sentence. A preposition can signal space and time (*above, below, near, after, before, until*) or exclusion (*except, but*).

SPACE	The smokestack is *near* the river.
TIME	They went home *after* the show.
EXCLUSION	Everyone *but* Mr. Kwan signed the petition.

There are fewer than one hundred prepositions in English. Some common prepositions are listed below.

about	before	during	off
above	behind	except	on
across	below	for	onto
after	beside	from	out
against	between	in	over
among	beyond	inside	past

around	by	into	toward
as	concerning	near	under
at	down	of	within

ESL NOTE: The frequently idiomatic use of prepositions presents special challenges for ESL learners. Depending on where you live in Canada, you may talk about going *into* town, *down*town, *up*town, or even *over* town.

23-g Articles

There are three **articles** in English—*a, an,* and *the*. An article works like an adjective in that it appears before a noun and indicates either a specific version or a generic version of that noun.

SPECIFIC   The children set *the* table.

GENERIC   We want to purchase *a* table.

The correct use of *a* and *an* depends on the initial sound, not letter, of the word that follows. *A* should be used before all words beginning with a consonant sound and a sounded *h*. *An* appears before words beginning with a vowel sound or a silent *h*.

a computer	an apple
a European	an MP
a historian	an uncle

ESL Focus — ARTICLES AND NOUNS

Articles can be a problem if your first language does not use articles before nouns. English uses articles in specific ways, some of which differ from how articles are used in other languages.

The article *the* precedes nouns that are specific; the articles *a* and *an* are used to mark nouns that are non-specific.

SPECIFIC   He is *the first* person to win the game.

NON-SPECIFIC   He saw *a person* enter the house.

WHEN TO USE *THE*	WHEN NOT TO USE AN ARTICLE
with names of countries that include such words as *kingdom, state, republic,* and union • the Republic of South Africa	with non-specific plural nouns and noncountable nouns • *Dogs* are good household pets; *rice* is a versatile staple food.
with plural proper nouns • the Rocky Mountains, the Toronto Maple Leafs, the United Nations, the Fongs	with singular proper nouns • John Smith, Dr. Mai Leung, Prime Minister Macdonald, Quebec
with names of oceans, seas, rivers, gulfs, canals, and deserts • the Atlantic, the Red River, the Sahara Desert	**Exception** • My Canada is a Canada that is tolerant of cultural diversity.
with names of languages and proper names that include *of* in their title • the English language, the University of Manitoba	with fields of study, names of diseases, and names of newspapers, magazines, and periodicals that do not have an article in the title • geography, measles, *Maclean's* magazine

23-h Interjections

Interjections are isolated words or phrases that express emotion. They can stand alone as complete sentences or they can be connected to another sentence. If connected to another sentence, they are usually set off by punctuation marks. Exclamation marks set off intense interjections, while commas are used for mild interjections.

Hey! What do you think you're doing?

Oh well, at least you tried.

A **phrase** is a group of words that functions as a noun, verb, or modifier; phrases cannot stand alone because they do not include both a subject (see 25-a) and a predicate (see 25-b). A **clause** is a group of words that contains both a subject and a predicate. There are two types of clauses: *dependent clauses*, which do not make a complete statement, and *independent clauses*, which do.

24-a Prepositional Phrases

The simplest building block in the English language beyond individual words is the **prepositional phrase**. A prepositional phrase consists of a preposition, its object, and any modifiers of the object. Although prepositional phrases usually function as adjectives or adverbs, they can function as subjects as well.

ADJECTIVE	I hear the sparrows *in the trees.*
ADVERB	*From their perches* they sing.
SUBJECT	*In the trees* seems a happy place to be.

24-b Verbal Phrases

Verb forms that function as modifiers and nouns rather than verbs are called verbals; they include present participles (the *-ing* form of a verb), past participles (the form of the verb ending in *-ed*, *-d*, *-en*, *-n*, or *-t*), and infinitives (the base form of a verb preceded by *to*). A **verbal phrase** consists of a verbal with any modifiers, objects, or complements. There are three kinds of verbal phrases: participial, gerund, and infinitive.

PARTICIPIAL PHRASES

Participial phrases contain either present participles or past participles, and always function as adjectives.

Canadians *travelling abroad* need a valid Canadian passport.

Drenched to the skin, Mai admitted she should have carried an umbrella.

GERUND PHRASES

Present participles (verbals ending in -*ing*) that function as nouns are called gerunds. A gerund phrase is made up of a gerund with any modifier, object, or complement.

> *Being a good student* is difficult. [subject of the verb]

INFINITIVE PHRASES

Infinitive phrases consist of an infinitive *(to see, to think, to kick, to be)* with any modifiers, objects, or complements. They can function as nouns, adjectives, or adverbs.

> *To be old* is a challenge. [subject of the verb]

> Travelling *to observe other cultures* can be an edifying experience. [adjective modifying *Travelling*]

> I laughed *to relieve my tension.* [adverb modifying *laughed*]

24-c Appositive Phrases

Appositives and appositive phrases identify or describe the nouns or pronouns that immediately precede them. The two types of appositives—restrictive and nonrestrictive—differ in their use of commas. A *restrictive appositive* is not set off with commas because it defines or limits the meaning of the noun or pronoun it names; it contains essential information and therefore could not be removed from the sentence. A *nonrestrictive appositive* is set off with commas because the information it contains is nonessential—that is, it expands on the meaning of the noun or pronoun but could be removed from the sentence without changing the basic meaning. (For more on commas and nonrestrictive elements, see 48-b.)

RESTRICTIVE	My younger sister *Tracy* is often afflicted with migraines. [The speaker has more than one sister.]
NONRESTRICTIVE	My sister, *Tracy,* is often afflicted with migraines. [Tracy is the speaker's only sister.]

24-d Absolute Phrases

Absolute phrases are made up of nouns and participles, together with any modifiers or objects. An absolute phrase modifies an entire sentence or clause and is set off from the rest of the sentence with commas.

Her voice shaking with anger, she dismissed him from her office.

24-e Independent Clauses

An **independent clause** is a group of words that contains both a *subject* and a *predicate* and can stand alone as a complete sentence.

The door is closed.

24-f Dependent Clauses

Dependent clauses (also known as *subordinate clauses*) contain both a *subject* and a *predicate* but cannot stand alone as complete sentences. A dependent clause functions within a sentence as an adverb, an adjective, or a noun.

ADVERB CLAUSES

Adverb clauses modify adjectives, adverbs, or words or groups of words that function as verbs. They begin with a subordinating conjunction and answer the questions *how, where, when,* or *why.*

When she reads the stock market report, Mel often finds new investment possibilities. [modifies a verb]

The victims of the home invasion recounted the terrifying incident calmly, *as if they were still in shock.*

[modifies another adverb]

ADJECTIVE CLAUSES

Adjective clauses (also known as *relative clauses*) modify nouns or pronouns. They begin with a relative pronoun (*who, whom, whose, whoever, whomever, that, which, whichever, what,* or *whatever)* or a relative adverb *(when, where, whether,* or *why).*

The boy *who won the free tickets to the concert* was standing right in front of the stage when his name was called. [relative pronoun as subject of clause]

The car *that was prominently featured in one of the early James Bond films* was an Aston Martin. [restrictive clause]

The reason *that Jack the Ripper committed his crimes* has eluded detectives for generations. [clause introduced by relative pronoun]

NOUN CLAUSES

Noun clauses function as subjects, direct objects, objects of prepositions, or subject complements. They begin with a relative pronoun *(who, whom, whose, whoever, whomever, that, which, whichever, what, whatever)* or with *when, where, whether, why,* or *how.* A noun clause can also function as an appositive and rename (identify or explain) a noun.

Whoever refuses to wear a seat belt courts disaster. [subject]

A business needs to know *what its customers want.* [direct object]

The mayoralty candidates scrambled for *whatever votes they could get.* [object of preposition]

The fact *that Mario had already seen the film* did not deter him from seeing it again. [appositive]

Sentence Elements

The two main parts of a sentence are the subject and the predicate.

25-a Subjects

The *simple subject* (SS) of a sentence is a noun or pronoun that carries out an action, is acted upon, or has something said about it.

> **SS**
> The *airplane* made an emergency landing.

A *complete subject* is made up of the simple subject and all the words that modify it.

> *The airplane with the damaged engine* made an emergency landing.

A *compound subject* consists of two or more simple subjects joined by a coordinating conjunction or a correlative conjunction. (For information about coordinating and correlative conjunctions, see 23-e.)

> *Harper and Mulcair* are political adversaries.

There are a variety of constructions in which the subject does not appear at the beginning of the sentence. In commands, the subject *you* is understood but not stated.

> **SS**
> [You] Get the ball!

> **SS**
> [You] Do your homework before watching TV!

In questions, the position of the subject changes.

> **SS**
> Why do *you* want to see that movie?

Sentences that begin with *there* can create confusion. *There* is not the subject of the sentence; it merely points to the subject that follows the verb.

SS
There is *Costa* over by the piano.

SS
There are *anchovies* on the pizza.

25-b Predicates

The *simple predicate* (SP) of a sentence is the main verb. A *complete predicate* consists of the main verb and its modifiers, together with any objects or complements and their modifiers.

────── COMPLETE PREDICATE ──────
  ⌐ SP
Patrick Chan *skated to a first-place finish at the 2013 World Championships.*

A *compound predicate* consists of two or more verbs that have the same subject and are joined by a coordinating conjunction or a correlative conjunction.

──────── COMPOUND PREDICATE ────────
  ⌐ SP   SP
Al *urged the company and advised the union to accept the deal.*

25-c Direct and Indirect Objects

A *direct object* (DO) is a word or word group that names the person or thing acted upon by the subject (S). It answers the questions *what?* or *whom?* about the verb (V).

    S   **V**   **DO**
The dog bit *the man.*

An *indirect object* (IO) is a noun or pronoun that answers the question *for whom?*, *to whom?*, *to what?*, or *for what?* about the verb.

    S   **V** **IO**   **DO**
Sam gave *you* the tickets.

When both objects are present in a sentence, the indirect object usually precedes the direct object.

IO ┌── DO ──┐
Marie-Claire lent *me the dictionary.*

EXCEPTIONS: The direct object precedes the indirect object (1) when the indirect object is placed in a prepositional phrase

┌── DO ──┐ ┌── IO ──┐
She sent *the package* to *her cousin.*

and (2) in sentences with the verbs *explain, describe, say, mention,* or *open.*

IO ┌── DO ──┐
INCORRECT   Loa explained *Signe the concept.*

┌── DO ──┐   IO
REVISED   Loa explained *the concept* to *Signe.*

25-d Subject and Object Complements

A *subject complement* (SC) is a word or word group that follows a *linking verb* (forms of *be* and verbs such as *seem, appear, become, grow, remain, stay, prove, feel, look, smell, sound,* and *taste*) and identifies or describes the subject.

┌── S ──┐   V ┌──── SC ────┐
The company remains *a solid investment.*

An *object complement* is a word or group that follows a direct object and identifies or describes that object.

S   V   DO ┌── OC ──
The reviewer pronounced the concert *an unmitigated disaster.*

26-a Pattern 1: Subject–Verb

The simplest sentence pattern you can use is the subject–verb pattern. All that is necessary to complete this pattern is a subject and an *intransitive verb* (the kind of verb that takes no object).

> S   V
> Birds fly.

> S   V
> Fish swim.

Building on this pattern does not change the basic structure of subject–verb.

> S   V
> Dogs bark frequently.

26-b Pattern 2: Subject–Verb–Direct Object

The verb in pattern 2 is the *transitive verb*, which transmits its action from a subject to an object.

> ⌐——S——⌐ ⌐—V—⌐ ⌐——DO——⌐
> The forward crosschecked the defenceman.

Think of the subject and transitive verb as asking the questions *who?* or *what?* and the direct object as answering either question.

Whom did the forward crosscheck? *The defenceman.*

26-c Pattern 3: Subject–Verb–Subject Complement

Pattern 3 uses a linking verb (forms of *be* and verbs such as *appear, become, feel, grow, look, make, seem, smell,* and *sound*) to connect a subject to its complement. A *subject complement* is a word or word group that identifies or describes the subject.

> ⌐—S—⌐ V   SC
> That pie smells delicious.

```
   S  V ┌─SC┐    S    V  ┌────── SC ──────┐
```
She is a lawyer.   He seems preoccupied today.

26-d Pattern 4: Subject–Verb–Indirect Object–Direct Object

Pattern 4 includes two objects: the direct object, which names the receiver of the action; and the indirect object, which identifies *to whom* or *to what* the action is done.

```
        S        V  ┌── IO──┐ ┌── DO──┐
```
The instructor assigns his students weekly tests.

26-e Pattern 5: Subject–Verb–Direct Object–Object Complement

Pattern 5 includes an object complement, which identifies or describes the direct object named by the transitive verb.

```
┌── S ──┐    V     DO   ┌──── OC ────┐
```
Some people consider taxpayers an overburdened
┌──┐
group.

27 SENTENCE TYPES

Grammatically, sentences are classified as *simple, compound, complex,* and *compound-complex.*

27-a Simple Sentences

A simple sentence consists of one independent clause with no dependent clauses. The subject and/or predicate of the independent clause may be compound.

Dick walked.

Until recently, Dick and Jane walked to the corner store and bought some candy every Saturday morning.

27-b Compound Sentences

A compound sentence consists of two or more independent clauses with no dependent clauses. It is therefore formed by coordination, with its two or more parts being equal. The clauses may be joined by a semicolon or by a comma and a coordinating conjunction *(and, but, or, nor, for, yet, so).*

┌INDEPENDENT CLAUSE ┐┌INDEPENDENT CLAUSE
They want to go to Australia, but they can't afford the airfare.

27-c Complex Sentences

A complex sentence is composed of one independent clause (IC) with at least one dependent clause (DC). When a dependent clause precedes the independent clause, as in the first example below, it is set off with a comma.

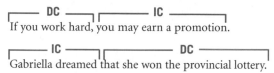

┌—— DC ——┐┌——— IC ———┐
If you work hard, you may earn a promotion.

┌——— IC ———┐┌——— DC ———┐
Gabriella dreamed that she won the provincial lottery.

The complex sentence is formed through subordination, with one clause placed in a subordinate relationship to another clause. Complex sentences allow you to communicate more complex relationships than the coordinate or equal relationships conveyed by compound sentences. Subordinating conjunctions introduce the dependent clauses in complex sentences. (For a list of common subordinating conjunctions, see page 174.)

27-d Compound-Complex Sentences

A compound-complex sentence consists of two or more independent clauses and at least one dependent clause.

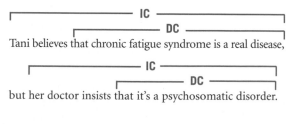

┌———————— IC ————————┐
  ┌———————— DC ———————┐
Tani believes that chronic fatigue syndrome is a real disease,

┌———————— IC ————————┐
  ┌———————— DC ———————┐
but her doctor insists that it's a psychosomatic disorder.

28 SENTENCE PURPOSES

28-a Classification

Sentences can be classified in terms of the purposes they fulfill. *Declarative* sentences make a statement, *interrogative* sentences ask a question, *imperative* sentences convey a command, and *exclamatory* sentences express strong emotion.

DECLARATIVE	In the 2012 Ryder Cup, the European team made a shocking come back on the last day to defeat the American team.
INTERROGATIVE	Did you see *Life of Pi*?
IMPERATIVE	Finish the report today.
EXCLAMATORY	What a sore loser she is!

28-b Formation of Interrogative Sentences

Interrogative sentences can be direct or indirect. A *direct question* asks a question directly and ends with a question mark. An *indirect question* is phrased differently: it reports rather than asks a question and is followed by a period.

DIRECT	Are the winters long in Winnipeg?
INDIRECT	She asked whether the winters were long in Winnipeg.

Declarative sentences with forms of the verb *to be (am, is, are, was,* and *were)* can be converted into direct questions by reversing the order of the subject and the verb.

DECLARATIVE	Increasing numbers of homeless people are sleeping on the street.
DIRECT	Are increasing numbers of homeless people sleeping on the street?

In direct questions that begin with *who, whom,* or *what,* the word order is determined by the case that is being used. If the subjective case is used, the subject *(who* or *what)* precedes the verb. If the objective case is used, the object *(whom* or *what)* appears before both the subject and the verb.

SUBJECTIVE	Who took the candy?
OBJECTIVE	Whom did the voters elect?

SENTENCE VARIETY 29

You can achieve variety in your writing by combining sentences, creating different sentence types, and making use of emphasis and contrast.

29-a Combining Sentence Elements

When you write, you are constantly creating relationships, assessing ideas, and determining priorities. In making these decisions, you are carrying out some of the basic planning and organizing of your work, but you are also determining whether an idea is coordinate (of equal value) or subordinate (of lesser value). This determination helps you to decide whether to combine particular sentence elements or leave them independent of each other.

Combining sentence elements can be as simple as joining subjects and predicates.

COMBINING SUBJECTS

Toronto has become a metropolis.

Montreal has become a metropolis.

Toronto and Montreal have become metropolises.

COMBINING PREDICATES

The football team runs the ball well.

The football team passes the ball well.

The football team runs and passes the ball well.

You can combine two independent clauses of equal importance by linking them with a comma and a coordinating conjunction *(and, but, so, for, or, nor, yet).*

```
        ┌──────────── INDEPENDENT CLAUSE ─────────┐
Kim Campbell was Canada's first female prime
└──────┘
minister,
```

```
        ┌─INDEPENDENT CLAUSE─┐
but she was in office very briefly.
```

If you were to decide that one independent clause is subordinate, you would rewrite it as a dependent clause.

```
        ┌──────────── DEPENDENT CLAUSE ───────────┐
Although Kim Campbell was Canada's first female
└────────────────┘
prime minister,
```

```
        ┌─ INDEPENDENT CLAUSE─┐
she was in office very briefly.
```

The most important point in the preceding example is the brevity of Campbell's tenure, *not* the fact that she was Canada's first female prime minister. Making Campbell's prime ministership the most important point would reverse the emphasis.

```
        ┌────── DEPENDENT CLAUSE ──────┐
Although she was in office very briefly,
```

```
        ┌────────── INDEPENDENT CLAUSE ──────────┐
Kim Campbell was Canada's first female prime
└──────┘
minister.
```

Instead of combining the two sentences about Campbell through either coordination or subordination, you could express the fact that Campbell was Canada's first female prime minister by using an appositive phrase (see 24-c). The appositive phrase in the following example makes the brevity of Campbell's tenure the more important point.

```
        ┌────── APPOSITIVE PHRASE ──────┐
Kim Campbell, Canada's first female prime minister,
was in office very briefly.
```

29-b Combining Sentences

The following passage consists of simple sentences. As you read the passage, notice how choppy the flow of ideas is.

TOO CHOPPY   Canada has many colourful place
                names. Some of them seem strange
                to us today. We do not remember

---

the origin of those names. Baie des Ha Ha, Quebec, is a good example. Ha Ha comes from the old French word for dead end: *haha*. Other places are named after events. According to legend, Medicine Hat, Alberta, is such a place. A Cree medicine man lost his headdress at Medicine Hat. He was fleeing the Blackfoot.

To eliminate the choppiness in this passage, you could combine the second and third sentences to create a compound sentence and join the last three sentences to form a complex sentence.

REVISED   Canada has many colourful place names. Some of them seem strange to us today, for we do not remember the origin of those names [*compound sentence*]. Baie des Ha Ha, Quebec, is a good example. Ha Ha comes from the old French word for dead end: *haha*. Other places are named after events. According to legend, Medicine Hat, Alberta, is the place where a Cree medicine man who was fleeing the Blackfoot lost his headdress [*complex sentence*].

29-c Establishing Emphasis and Contrast

One way to keep your readers engaged is to introduce emphasis and contrast into your sentences. You can do so by *varying the lengths of your sentences, using periodic sentences where appropriate,* and *creating parallel structures.*

VARYING SENTENCE LENGTHS

The following passage consists of seven short sentences and a concluding long sentence. The long sentence derives much of its power from the contrast between its length and that of the sentences that precede it.

When he arrived in Ottawa, Stephen Harper puzzled veteran political observers. He was composed in personal presentation, conservative in dress, and careful in speech. He lacked the more immediately apparent magnetism of a Layton or a Chrétien. At press conferences, he stressed fact and precedent and detail rather than emotion. His common facial expression was limited to serious concern. He seemed a man born to wear a dark suit. He rarely joked or laughed aloud in public. *Behind this composed surface, however, lived the man who had succeeded in doing what more experienced political figures had failed to do—unite the conservative forces in Canada behind a single party.*

Equally effective is the next passage, in which the concluding short sentence is preceded by three long sentences.

Aside from a shared living space, what do the following species have in common—Atlantic cod, monkfish, bluefin tuna, rockfish, Atlantic salmon? If you answered that they are all on the list of fish we should avoid buying because their numbers are dangerously low, you are right. It is hard to get people to worry about a species as long as they keep appearing in stores for sale. It is also hard to get people to worry about fish when they are farmed in different areas of the world. But we are the people who virtually exterminated the most abundant species of fish ever known in Canada and made Newfoundlanders turn to fishing for oil instead of cod. *We need to start worrying.*

LOOSE AND PERIODIC SENTENCES

A loose or cumulative sentence begins with the subject and the predicate and then accumulates information as it progresses.

LOOSE	*The ferry gently nosed into the dock,* the line of its journey still visible in its broadening wake.

In contrast, a periodic sentence builds to its main idea by not revealing the subject and predicate until the end.

PERIODIC	The line of its journey still visible in its broadening wake, *the ferry gently nosed into the dock.*

PARALLELISM

Parallelism in a sentence is created by repeating grammatical elements, whether words, phrases, or entire clauses. Parallel structures give your writing a special kind of emphasis because they contain both repeating elements and changing elements. See how the phrase *They worried that* in the passage about the Toronto Maple Leafs establishes a repeating (or parallel) element and grants extra emphasis to the parts of the sentence that are different.

> In the 2012–2013 season, the Toronto Maple Leafs, after years of mediocre performance and consignment to the bottom half of the Eastern Conference, were worried heading into the NHL season. *They worried that,* again, the opposition teams would score the timely and winning goals, get the quality of goaltending that single-handedly wins games, and generate the points necessary to qualify for the playoffs. *They worried that,* no matter how much effort they put into the last half of the season, they would be golfing while players on other teams excited their fans with playoff victories. They worried needlessly.

For more information about parallelism, see 33-c and 39-d.

Constructing Paragraphs

The key qualities of a successful paragraph are *unity, coherence,* and *emphasis.* A unified paragraph focuses on a single subject or idea, while a coherent paragraph gains its unity from the linking of its sentences as they address that subject. Emphasis refers to the means the writer employs to engage and maintain the reader's interest, to make the paragraph not only informative but also clear and memorable. To write an effective paragraph, you need to know what the purpose of the paragraph is and how best to accomplish that purpose.

30 SEQUENCING IDEAS

Some of the most common ways to sequence the ideas in a paragraph are these:

- from general to specific
  - topic to illustration
  - problem to solution
  - claim to support for claim
- from specific to general
  - illustration to topic
- from least important or complex to most important or complex
- from most important or familiar to least important or familiar
- according to time
- according to space

Part of your understanding of sequencing may come from the sorting activities (listing, mind-mapping, branching, outlining, and so forth) that you engage in during the prewriting stage. When constructing a paragraph, you need to decide what the paragraph's *main claim* (or thesis) is and how it relates to the rest of the paragraph. You typically present the main claim in your paragraph's *lead* or *topic sentence.* Although the main claim may appear in the middle of your paragraph, it typically comes at the beginning or end.

Ask yourself what the intent of your paragraph is. How does it relate to the paragraphs that precede and follow it? What transitions or links do you need to connect it to those paragraphs or to your topic? Your answers to these questions help you decide whether you want to start with your main claim and then support it with details or whether you want to start with one or more details and move to your main claim.

PARAGRAPH PURPOSE 31

One of the keys to writing is to keep your purpose in mind. A paragraph's pattern of organization will largely depend on the paragraph's purpose. Just as sentences can introduce, claim, argue, add detail, illustrate, define, evaluate, review, connect, or conclude, so too can paragraphs. Ideally, a paragraph serves both a specific local purpose—to define, claim, or provide an example—and a general purpose—to advance or suggest the essay's major claim.

PARAGRAPH DEVELOPMENT 32

There are a variety of different patterns of organization you can use to develop your paragraphs. This section introduces eight developmental modes: *narration, description, exposition, example, explanation, classification and division, comparison and contrast,* and *definition.*

32-a Narration

A *narrative paragraph* tells you what happened or what is happening. To test the effectiveness of a narrative paragraph, ask the following questions:

- Is the illustration relevant or connected directly to the claim?
- Is the passage organized chronologically?

- Does the narrative show a cause-and-effect relationship between events?
- Is the lead or topic sentence the key to understanding the narrative?

32-b Description

A *descriptive paragraph* sketches a portrait of a person, an object, or an event. To test the effectiveness of a descriptive paragraph, ask these questions:

- Are the description's various elements logically arranged?
- Do the primary elements of the description stand out?
- Does the description express a clear, dominant point of view?

32-c Exposition

Expository writing is writing that analyzes, that deals with ideas and engages the reader through its appeal to reason. The writing you do in postsecondary courses typically asks you to inform, persuade, or analyze in addressing a subject assigned to you. The most common structure of an *academic paragraph* is the stating of a claim and the use of reasoning to support that claim. The claim can be made early or late in the paragraph, but reasoned support must be offered in defence of the claim.

32-d Example or Illustration

An *example* or *illustration paragraph* uses a specific example to illustrate a point. In such a paragraph, the example should be clearly stated and the point it is illustrating should be a valid one. An example paragraph must use specific details to develop its illustration in a clear, compelling, and concrete way.

32-e Explanation

An *explanatory paragraph* explores its subject by breaking it into its constituent parts and describing those parts. The writer uses analysis to separate the whole into parts. Another way to write an explanation is to use *process* or

---

analogy. A recipe is a common example of an explanation using process. Analogy uses a simpler or more familiar experience to help the reader understand an unfamiliar concept or process.

32-f Classification and Division

Classification groups items into categories on the basis of a unifying principle. *Division* takes a single item and breaks it into parts.

32-g Comparison and Contrast

When you *compare* two topics, you draw attention to their similarities. When you *contrast* two topics, you highlight their differences. A comparison and/or contrast paragraph may be structured in one of two ways. You may present information about one topic first and follow this with information about the other topic. Alternatively, you may move back and forth between the two topics, focusing on particular aspects.

32-h Definition

A *definition paragraph* establishes the meaning of a word or a concept. Writers sometimes assume this simply means transferring a definition from a dictionary to the essay's page. But a definition paragraph deals with a stipulative definition, that is, what the writer takes a word or concept to mean. For a definition to occupy an entire paragraph, the subject is normally a complex one. We write a definition paragraph when we have to explain clearly to our readers what a term or concept means. We may draw on example, history, contrast/comparison, even geography, for that definition.

32-i Causal Analysis

A *causal analysis* paragraph traces the reason why an event or a process occurred. Often, the causal chain is longer than a single paragraph could cover, so an individual paragraph will trace only one constituent of that causal chain. For more on causal analysis, see page 13.

The connections between the sentences that make up a paragraph should be clear and logical. Transitions contribute to the coherence of a paragraph by indicating the precise relationships between sentences. Transitional devices include *transitional expressions, repetition,* and *parallel structure.*

33-a Transitional Expressions

Transitional expressions are words or phrases that signal the connections between sentences. As the following list indicates, transitional expressions perform a variety of functions.

TO ADD

additionally, also, and, as well, besides, further, furthermore, in addition, moreover, too

TO GIVE AN EXAMPLE

for example, for instance, indeed, in fact, namely, specifically, such as, to illustrate

TO INDICATE CLARIFICATION

in other words, simply put, that is, to clarify, to put it simply

TO INDICATE SEQUENCE

afterward, and then, before, finally, first (second, third), following, immediately, in the first place, last, next

TO EMPHASIZE OR FOCUS

above all, even, indeed, in fact, in particular, more importantly, obviously, of course, specifically, that is, truly

TO COMPARE

again, also, by the same token, in the same manner, in the same way, just as . . . so too, likewise, similarly

TO CONTRAST

although, but, conversely, despite, even though, however, in contrast, in spite of, instead, nevertheless, nonetheless, notwithstanding, on the contrary, on the other hand, rather, still, though, whereas, yet

TO INDICATE CONCESSION

admittedly, although it is true that, granted that, naturally, of course, to be sure

TO INDICATE TIME

after, after a while, afterward, as, as long as, as soon as, at last, at that time, at this point, before, currently, during, earlier, eventually, finally, formerly, immediately, in the future, in the meantime, in the past, lately, later, meanwhile, next, now, presently, recently, shortly, simultaneously, since, so far, soon, subsequently, temporarily, then, thereafter, until, when, while

TO INDICATE PLACE OR DIRECTION

above, adjacent to, around, behind, below, beyond, close to, elsewhere, farther on, here, inside, near, nearby, opposite, there, to the left, to the right, under, underneath

TO INDICATE CAUSE AND EFFECT

accordingly, as a result, because, consequently, due to, for this purpose, for this reason, hence, since, so, then, therefore, thereupon, thus, to this end

TO REPEAT, SUMMARIZE, OR CONCLUDE

after all, all in all, all told, altogether, as a result, as mentioned, as noted, finally, hence, in brief, in conclusion, in other words, in short, in summary, in the final analysis, on the whole, that is, therefore, thus, to conclude, to summarize, to sum up

33-b Repetition

Less common than the use of transitional expressions is the use of repetition to create transitions within paragraphs. The repeated element, which may be a word or phrase, functions as the paragraph's connective tissue.

33-c Parallel Structure

Parallel structures—a series of words, phrases, or clauses that have the same grammatical function—bring coherence to a paragraph by emphasizing the connections between ideas.

For information about faulty parallel structure, see 39-d.

In the initial stages of constructing a paragraph, you are probably more concerned with clarifying your purpose and articulating your ideas than with deciding how your paragraph should be structured. You can increase the range of your composing choices, however, by becoming familiar with the structural patterns discussed in this section.

34-a The Levels Concept

The concept of *levels* in paragraphs was introduced by the American composition theorist Francis Christensen.[1] This concept issues from the fact that, in successful paragraphs, a sentence is a single unit of development. It cannot function on its own, however, and is necessarily connected to what comes before it and to what comes after. Christensen saw that a paragraph is created by combining sentences on different levels. The lead or topic sentence of a paragraph—the *level-one sentence* in Christensen's terms—contains the most general observation made in that paragraph about the paragraph's topic. A *level-two sentence* is a sentence that develops, in more detail, some part of what was said in the level-one sentence. A *level-three sentence* develops some aspect of what was conveyed in a level-two sentence. This feature of continuing subordination can lead, naturally, to further levels.

Christensen argued that every sentence in a paragraph is either subordinate or coordinate. A sentence that relates to the sentence immediately preceding it performs a *subordinate* function by developing more precisely some aspect of that sentence. A sentence that relates to the lead sentence is *coordinate* with the other sentences in the paragraph that relate to that lead sentence. When the first sentence of a paragraph is the paragraph's lead sentence, the second sentence can be either subordinate or coordinate depending on its connection to the first sentence.

When you reason in your writing, Christensen observed, you do so principally by the methods of coordination and subordination. In coordination, a series of

---

[1] See Francis Christensen, "A Generative Rhetoric of the Paragraph," in W. Ross Winterowd, ed., *Contemporary Rhetoric: A Conceptual Background with Readings* (New York: Harcourt Brace Jovanovich, 1975), 233–52.

sentences develops a general observation; in subordination, each sentence represents a more detailed or exact development of an observation, image, or insight in the preceding sentence. Frequently, both coordination and subordination are used in a paragraph.

34-b Coordinate, Subordinate, and Mixed Structures

Christensen's analysis showed that it is possible to use three kinds of paragraph structures: *coordinate, subordinate,* and *mixed.* You can see how these structures work by examining the paragraphs that follow. In each paragraph, the number preceding each sentence denotes the level of that sentence.

COORDINATE STRUCTURE

(1) The paragraph, as a composing unit, has been affected by three principal influences in the last century. (2) First, it has been shortened by the advent of mass printing and publication and the commercial wish to please everyone. (2) Second, it has simplified its diction considerably, partly because of a shift in taste and style, partly because of an increasing uncertainty about the abilities of the mass reader. (2) Finally, it has increasingly resorted to artificial modes of emphasis in an attempt to sustain the reader's attention.

SUBORDINATE STRUCTURE

(1) The paragraph, a basic unit of composition, was severely influenced by the mass-production methods that came to dominate publishing in the last century. (2) Because the intended audience had increased tenfold and now included the barely literate as well as the rhetorically sophisticated, the paragraph grew shorter and shorter. (3) This condensing of average paragraph length was most notable in newspapers, where the narrow width of columns obscured the fact that most paragraphs had only a few sentences. (4) You should not be surprised, therefore, to learn that the average modern paragraph is less than half the length of a nineteenth-century paragraph.

MIXED STRUCTURE

(1) The paragraph, as a composing unit, has been affected by three principal influences in the last century. (2) It has been shortened by the advent of mass printing and publication and a wish to please everyone. (3) This shortening, gradual in the last part of the nineteenth century and the first quarter of the twentieth, was accelerated by Hemingway's example and the increasing influence of journalism. (2) The paragraph has also seen its diction simplified. (3) This can be attributed to shifts in both taste and style. (4) Certainly, the belief that plain speaking was honest speaking contributed to the dominance of a simpler vocabulary in the paragraph. (2) Finally, the paragraph came to cultivate increasingly artificial means of emphasis. (3) This is sharply evident in magazines appealing to teens where block letters, multiple exclamation marks, and direct, intimate address create a synthetically appealing style.

Christensen observed that the first sentence of a paragraph was frequently the lead or topic sentence, since the other sentences depended on it. He also discovered that the most common structure in paragraphs is the mixed sequence, in which both coordinate and subordinate patterns are used. Perhaps the most important truth demonstrated by Christensen's model is that all sentences in a paragraph must be connected in some way if your readers are to grasp your intentions.

35 SPECIAL-PURPOSE PARAGRAPHS

In an essay, certain paragraphs perform unique tasks. The most important of these special-purpose paragraphs are introductory paragraphs, transitional paragraphs, and concluding paragraphs.

35-a Introductory Paragraphs

The first paragraph of an essay is probably the most demanding of all to write. In the opening paragraph, you must introduce your topic and at the same time capture the attention or interest of your readers. You have the option in this paragraph of giving your readers a clear sense of the direction of your essay. These three functions are fulfilled by means of the hook, the thesis statement (or claim), and the preview.

HOOK

The term *hook* comes from the world of television. Scriptwriters in that medium must establish a strong opening to discourage channel-surfing. As an essayist, you have a similar objective when composing your introductory paragraph. Techniques you can use to hook your readers include the following: a provocative quotation, an engaging anecdote, a powerful description, a strong statement, a memorable example, a thought-provoking question, and an intriguing fact or statistic. All of these techniques or hooks must, of course, relate in some way to your topic.

THESIS STATEMENT

A key element of the opening paragraph is the thesis statement or claim, a single sentence that conveys your essay's central point or idea. Opening paragraphs typically move from the general to the specific, concluding with the most specific sentence in the paragraph—the thesis. In such a construction, general statements lead to more specific statements and all of these prepare readers for the thesis statement.

PREVIEW

If you wish to give your readers a clear understanding of the direction your essay will take, you can include a preview in your opening paragraph. This element is optional. In an argument, for instance, you may elect not to present a preview because you may want your points, and the conclusion(s) you draw from them, to surprise the reader. A preview typically follows the thesis statement or claim.

35-b Transitional Paragraphs

Transitional paragraphs are used to signal a major transition between ideas. A transitional paragraph typically performs three tasks: summarizing, emphasizing, and previewing. It may also provide background on a subject.

The following excerpt from Sally Armstrong's essay "Veiled Threats: The Women of Afghanistan" illustrates how a transitional paragraph (shown here in italics) can knit together a narrative.

> There are 30,000 widows in Kabul who are virtually destitute. When asked how they should cope, the Taliban reply again, "Let them die." In a particularly hateful response to the handicapped, some men have told their disabled wives that they'll no longer require prostheses as they no longer need to be seen outside.
>
> *Afghanistan is a country about the size of Manitoba. It has five major tribes that have warred endlessly throughout the centuries. It was a monarchy until 1972 and a republic until 1978 when the Soviets invaded. Then it became one of the last violent crucibles of the Cold War. The detested boot camp rule of the Soviets spawned the Mujahideen (Freedom Fighter) camps across the border in Northern Pakistan. . . . Life under the victorious Mujahideen proved to be as violent as it had been under the Communists and more religiously strict than the people had ever imagined. Enter the Taliban, young hoodlums who had never been to school and never known anything but war. Presently they control two-thirds of the country.*
>
> While the world has clearly grown weary of Afghanistan and its 18 years of war, the people trapped in that country and the 500,000 refugees who escaped to border towns in Northern Pakistan are hoping someone will "take up our quarrel with the foe." Although the Taliban have no official role in the Islamic Republic of Pakistan, their presence throughout the north is threatening.*
>
> — Sally Armstrong, "Veiled Threats: The Women of Afghanistan"

---

*Excerpt from *The Veiled Threat: The Hidden Power of the Women of Afghanistan*, by Sally Armstrong. © Sally Armstrong.

35-c Concluding Paragraphs

The final paragraph of an essay fulfills three basic functions:

1. It summarizes the essay's key points.
2. It restates the claim or thesis.
3. It indicates the general significance of the claim or thesis.

In addition, a concluding paragraph should strike a note of finality; it should leave readers with the impression that nothing of importance has been left unsaid.

Concluding paragraphs usually follow a specific-to-general pattern (the reverse of the general-to-specific pattern typical of introductory paragraphs). See how Geoffrey Bibby finishes his essay on the work of archaeologists:

> Further we cannot go. We have been probing, with our picks and shovels and builder's trowels, not merely into the brains but perhaps also into the souls of men, and we must be content if our diagnosis is imprecise and inconclusive. But it does take us a little way beyond the conventional archaeological picture of the material lives of the simple peasants of barbarian Europe. Behind the material life, interleaved with it and perhaps dominating it, was the world of taboos and magic and superstition, the spirits of the earth and the heavens, who had to be bribed or placated or bought off. One of the occupational risks of Iron Age Europe, right up to the end of the Viking period scarcely a thousand years ago, was that of being chosen as victim, as the price to be paid for prosperity in the next harvest or victory in the next war. It was only with the coming of Christianity that human sacrifice ceased in Europe; looking on the bodies from the Danish bogs we should do well to realize that there, but for the grace of God, lie we.

> — Geoffrey Bibby, "The Body in the Bog"

A number of factors can reduce the effectiveness of your paragraphs. Here are the most common pitfalls:

- undefined purpose or thesis
- lack of coherence
- wordy expression
- extraneous detail
- inappropriate example
- poor organization
- lack of unity
- confusing or missing transitions

Grammatical Sentences

A sentence is an independent clause, a group of words that contains both a subject and a predicate. The subject names the thing or person that the sentence is about; it is acted upon by the verb. The predicate consists of the verb and any object, modifier, or complement of the verb. (For more information about subjects and predicates, see 25-a and 25-b.)

┌─ **SUBJECT** ─┬┌──────── **PREDICATE** ──────────
Grey's Anatomy depicts the personal traumas of the
staff of a metropolitan hospital.

37-a Sentence Fragments

A sentence fragment is a word group that, for various reasons, fails to qualify as a sentence. For example, there may be no subject or no predicate.

NO SUBJECT	Having crossed the Pacific. [Who crossed the Pacific?]
NO PREDICATE	The first Chinese, who came to Canada from California in 1858. [What did the Chinese do?]

In a third kind of fragment, both a subject and a predicate are present, but they are preceded by a subordinating conjunction.

After Cirque du Soleil started to become popular in the United States. [What happened after it started to become popular?]

CORRECTING SENTENCE FRAGMENTS

A fragment that lacks a *subject* can be corrected by adding a subject or by combining the fragment with an independent clause.

FRAGMENT	Having crossed the Pacific.
REVISED	Having crossed the Pacific, the first known Japanese immigrant to Canada settled in Victoria in 1877. [combined with independent clause]

A fragment that lacks a *predicate* can be corrected by adding a predicate or by combining the fragment with an independent clause.

FRAGMENT   The first Chinese, who came
                        to Canada from California in
                        1858.

REVISED   The first Chinese, who came
                        to Canada from California in
                        1858, were looking for gold
                        on the Fraser River. [predicate
                        added]

ESL Focus   MISSING SUBJECTS AND VERBS

You may be familiar with a language that allows the omission of an explicit subject or verb if the sentence is clear without it. Such an omission is not permitted in English, however. For that reason, the following examples are fragments, not sentences.

MISSING SUBJECT   Has asked for plans for two
                  new parks.

MISSING VERB   The Grey Cup in Vancouver in
                  2014.

MISSING VERB   Winnipeggers very outgoing.

To revise these fragments, add the subjects and verbs required to complete the sentence.

City council
  Has asked for plans for two new parks.
^

        will be held
The Grey Cup in Vancouver in 2014.
            ^

            are
Winnipeggers very outgoing.
            ^

EXCEPTION: The imperative sentence, which expresses a command, need not include a stated subject. For example, in the sentence *Clean up your room,* the subject *You* is assumed, not stated.

If the fragment is a phrase or a dependent clause, either combine it with an independent clause or turn it into an independent clause.

FRAGMENT	In 1870 by the Icelandic community.
REVISED	In Manitoba, women's suffrage was first proposed in 1870 by the Icelandic community. [phrase combined with an independent clause]

Most fragmented dependent clauses are partial thoughts that have been unintentionally separated from a nearby sentence where they belong. To correct such fragments, simply join the two parts.

FRAGMENT	Canadian women felt cheated. When the federal government extended voting rights in 1917 only to women in the armed services and to female relatives of men in the military.
REVISED	Canadian women felt cheated when, in 1917, the federal government extended voting rights only to women in the armed services and to female relatives of men in the military.

ESL Focus   VERBAL-PHRASE FRAGMENTS

A special type of fragment results when the writer assumes that a verbal phrase can function as a verb.

FRAGMENT	The candidate, *having learned* that he was trailing in the polls, and *knowing* that he would have a hard time catching up in the last week.

continued

You may think the above example is a complete sentence because it contains words that sound like verbs. However, *having learned* and *knowing* are verbals, not verbs. The clause has a subject (*the candidate*) but no predicate because it has no verb; it does not tell its readers what the candidate *did* after learning he was trailing in the polls. Changing a verbal phrase to a verb or adding a predicate will correct the unintended fragment.

REVISED *The candidate,* having learned that he was trailing in the polls, and knowing that he would have a hard time catching up in the last week, *launched a series of hard-hitting television advertisements.*

37-b Run-On Sentences

Run-on sentences consist of independent clauses that have not been joined correctly. They fall into two categories: the *fused sentence* and the *comma splice.*

FUSED SENTENCES

When two independent clauses are joined with no punctuation or connecting word between them, the result is a fused sentence.

FUSED SENTENCE Constance loves to read she often falls asleep at night with a book pressed to her nose.

To correct a fused sentence, you have the following options:

1. Make the two independent clauses into separate sentences.

    Constance loves to read. She often falls asleep at night with a book pressed to her nose.

2. Link the clauses with a comma and a coordinating conjunction *(and, but, yet, or, for, nor, so)*.

> Constance loves to read, *and* she often falls asleep at night with a book pressed to her nose.

3. Link the clauses with a semicolon or with a semicolon followed by a conjunctive adverb.

> Constance loves to read; *consequently,* she often falls asleep at night with a book pressed to her nose.

4. Turn one of the independent clauses into a dependent clause.

> Because Constance loves to read, she often falls asleep at night with a book pressed to her nose.

5. Turn the two clauses into a single independent clause.

> Constance's passion for reading sometimes causes her to fall asleep at night with a book pressed to her nose.

COMMA SPLICES

A comma splice occurs when two independent clauses are joined with only a comma.

COMMA SPLICE   Yann Martel's novel *Life of Pi* was a critical and popular success, it was made into a movie.

The methods for eliminating comma splices are the same as those for correcting fused sentences.

38-a Subject–Verb Agreement

A verb must agree with its subject in number (singular or plural) and in person (first, second, or third).

	SINGULAR	PLURAL
FIRST PERSON	I see	we see
SECOND PERSON	you see	you see
THIRD PERSON	he/she/it sees	they see

SUBJECTS WITH *AND*

Most compound subjects joined by *and* are plural and therefore require a plural verb.

> *are*
> Geneviève and Cloë ~~is~~ going to the dance next Saturday.

Two linked subjects that are viewed as a single unit take a singular verb.

> *is*
> Strawberries and cream ~~are~~ Marsha's favourite dessert.

WORDS OR PHRASES BETWEEN SUBJECT AND VERB

Words or phrases that come between the subject and the verb can cause confusion.

> *was*
> *One* of the students ~~were~~ writing a report on the effectiveness of Canada's policy on multiculturalism.

In the preceding example, the subject is *one*, not *students*. *Students* is part of the phrase *of the students*, which modifies the noun (and subject) *one*. The verb must agree with *one*; only one student is writing the report.

When a singular subject is followed by a phrase beginning with *as well as, in addition to, together with,* or a similar construction, the verb should agree with the singular subject, not with the subject in the intervening phrase.

Gordon, together with his classmates, ~~think~~ *thinks* Arnold Schwarzenegger's best acting occurred during his time as the governor of California.

SUBJECTS JOINED BY *OR* OR *NOR*

When a compound subject is joined by *or* or *nor*, make the verb agree with the part of the subject closest to the verb.

Customs or *tradition shapes* everyday behaviour.

Tradition or *customs shape* everyday behaviour.

When a singular subject and a plural subject are joined by *either/or* or *neither/nor,* you can avoid awkwardness by placing the plural subject closest to the verb.

| AWKWARD | Neither the *students* nor the *instructor is* happy that the classroom is too hot. |
| REVISED | Neither the *instructor* nor the *students are* happy that the classroom is too hot. |

INDEFINITE PRONOUNS AS SUBJECTS

Indefinite pronouns, such as *one, none, each, either, neither, another, anyone,* and *anything,* refer to non-specific persons or things and are singular in meaning. The indefinite pronouns *everyone, everybody,* and *everything* are also singular even though they appear to be plural in meaning.

Everyone ~~are~~ *is* disappointed that a Canadian team has not captured the Stanley Cup since Montreal won it in 1993.

Some indefinite pronouns, including *all, any,* and *some,* can be either singular or plural, depending on the noun they refer to.

| SINGULAR | *Some* of the instructor's *lesson* is hard to understand. |
| PLURAL | *Some instructors* are hard to understand. |

COLLECTIVE NOUNS AS SUBJECTS

Collective nouns, such as *class, family, team, committee, audience, couple,* and *group,* can take either a singular or a plural verb, depending on whether they function as a single unit or as individual members of a unit.

| SINGULAR | The *jury has* returned a verdict of guilty. [functions as single unit] |
| PLURAL | The *jury are* debating the evidence. [function as individual members of unit] |

The names of companies are collective nouns. Most company names with plural or compound forms take singular verbs.

Chapters *is* seeking to expand its customer base.

SUBJECT COMPLEMENTS

A verb should agree with the subject, not with the subject complement.

were
Excessive absences ~~was~~ the reason for the employee's dismissal.

In the preceding example sentence, the plural subject *absences* is linked to the singular complement *reason* by the plural verb *were*. If the subject and complement in this sentence were reversed, the verb would be singular.

was
The reason for the employee's dismissal ~~were~~ excessive absences.

For more information about subject complements, see 25-d.

INTRODUCTORY *THERE*

In sentences beginning with *There*, the number of the verb depends on the subject that follows *There*.

There *is* a *flaw* in Monique's design.

There *are* several *flaws* in Monique's design.

ESL Focus | **NONCOUNTABLE NOUNS AND GERUNDS**

Singular verbs are used with noncountable nouns and gerunds.

NONCOUNTABLE NOUN   The *information* is inaccurate.

GERUND   *Winning* is fun.

For more information about noncountable nouns, see the ESL Focus in 23-a.

WHO, THAT, WHICH

Verbs in dependent clauses introduced by the relative pronouns *who, that,* and *which* must agree with the antecedents of these relative pronouns.

The *Stoneys,* who *are* related to the Plains Assiniboine, traditionally lived along the foothills of the Rocky Mountains.

The *language* that *is* native to the Stoneys is a dialect of the Siouan language spoken by the Sioux.

PLURAL FORM, SINGULAR MEANING

Some nouns ending in *-s* are singular in meaning and therefore take singular verbs.

is
Mathematics ~~are~~ an essential skill.

Some of these nouns may be either singular or plural depending on the context.

SINGULAR   Statistics *is* the most challenging course in the new curriculum.

PLURAL   His statistics *are* accurate.

In the singular example above, *statistics* denotes a field of study; in the plural example, it refers to a collection of specific information.

Words referred to as words or terms take singular verbs.

> *Councillors* ~~are~~ *is* a term that is gender-neutral.

PHRASES OF MEASURE AND QUALITY

Units of money, time, volume, mass, length, and distance take singular verbs.

> Two kilometres ~~are~~ *is* the equivalent of a mile and a quarter.

TITLES OF WORKS

The title of a book, film, or other work of art takes a singular verb even if the title has a plural or compound form.

> Tomson Highway's *The Rez Sisters* ~~were~~ *was* first produced at the Native Canadian Centre of Toronto in 1986.

38-b Tense Agreement

Verb tenses should clearly establish the time of the actions being described in a sentence or a passage. Tenses should be changed only when the context requires a shift.

> The belief that Quebec is the most highly taxed region in North America *is* patently untrue. Yet this popular myth about Quebec ~~perpetuated~~ *perpetuates* itself.

Problems with tenses can occur when quotations are used to support commentary.

> Vanderhaeghe's *The Englishman's Boy* focuses in part on the battle that took place in the Cypress Hills in southwestern Saskatchewan in 1873. Vanderhaeghe comments specifically on the fact that those responsible for the massacre of Native people

included both Americans and Canadians. Yet,

makes
Vanderhaeghe ~~made~~ another point at the end of his
novel when he writes that, as a result of the incident,
"The Canadian government formed the North West
Mounted Police, sent it on a long, red-jacketed march
into a vast territory, establishing claim to it. A mythic
act of possession" (326).

In the sentence leading into the quotation, *made* has been
changed to *makes* because the present tense is used in the
commentary that precedes the quotation. Besides making
the verb tense consistent with the tense of the rest of the
paragraph, it also follows the literary convention of utilizing the present tense in analyzing a literary work.

38-c Pronoun–Antecedent Agreement

Pronouns are words that replace nouns (see 23-b). A pronoun must agree with its antecedent—the word it replaces—
in *number*, *gender*, and *person*.

The injured Canadian *soldiers* learned that *their*
pensions would no longer be affected by *their*
disability payments.

COMPOUND ANTECEDENTS

When the parts of a compound antecedent are joined by
and, the matching pronoun is plural.

Lady Gaga and Norah Jones have forged *their*
individual careers in remarkably different ways.

A compound antecedent that is preceded by *each* or *every*
requires a singular pronoun.

Each car and truck must meet stringent air-pollution
standards before *it* is allowed on the road.

When a compound antecedent is joined by *or* or *nor*, the pronoun agrees with the nearest antecedent.

> Neither the *manager* nor her *employees* are happy about *their* new assignment.

INDEFINITE PRONOUNS

When the antecedent is an indefinite pronoun whose meaning is singular, the matching pronoun is singular.

> *One* of the hockey players lost *his* temper.

When the antecedent is an indefinite pronoun whose meaning is plural, the matching pronoun is plural.

> *Many* of the victorious teammates raised *their* arms in jubilation.

When the antecedent is an indefinite pronoun whose meaning can be singular or plural (e.g., *all, any, none,* and *some*), the matching pronoun is singular or plural depending on the noun it refers to.

> SINGULAR   *Some* of the *art* appealed to *its* viewers.
>
> PLURAL   *Some* of the *politicians* have broken *their* campaign promises.

Indefinite pronouns, such as *one, anyone, someone, each, everybody, no one,* and *nobody,* raise the problem of sexist bias when they are matched with a singular pronoun that is exclusionary and sexist.

> EXCLUSIONARY   *Everybody* has to buy *his* own books.

To avoid exclusion, you can use both masculine and feminine pronouns.

> REVISED   *Everyone* has to buy *his* or *her* own books.

Alternatively, you can replace the indefinite pronoun with a plural noun.

> REVISED   *Students* have to buy *their* own books.

See Chapter 44 for a more detailed discussion of inclusive language.

ESL Focus GENDER AND AGREEMENT

The gender of nouns and pronouns varies from language to language and from culture to culture. The two major languages in Canada, French and English, use gender in quite different ways. In French, pronouns and the nouns they replace are either masculine or feminine. In English, many constructions are gender-neutral.

- The *cat* rolled on *its* back.
- The *tree* shaded the cat with *its* branches.

Nouns that are gender-specific include *bull, cow, stag, doe, gander, goose, lady, lord, prince, princess, man,* and *woman.*

38-d Person Agreement

Do not shift among first, second, and third person unless meaning demands it. The following passage illustrates awkward and unnecessary shifts in person:

AWKWARD   If *people* go to a movie theatre on the weekend, *they* will probably encounter large lineups for the most popular films. *I* may even end up going to a film *I* did not intend, or want, to see. To ensure that *you* see the film of your choice, *you* should arrive early.

In the passage, the writer shifts from the third-person noun and pronoun *(people/they)*, to the first-person pronoun *(I)*, to the second-person pronoun *(you)*. The problems of clarity and logic are easily solved by eliminating the person agreement problems.

REVISED   If *you* go to a movie theatre on the weekend, *you* will probably encounter large lineups for the most popular films. *You* may even end up going to a film *you* did not intend, or want, to see. To ensure that *you* see the film of your choice, *you* should arrive early.

39-a Unclear Pronoun Reference

Pronouns that do not refer clearly to their antecedents are common sources of confusion for readers. A pronoun reference is ambiguous when the pronoun could refer to more than one antecedent.

> **AMBIGUOUS** Roger told Samarjit that he was being transferred to Montreal.

As the following revisions indicate, there are two possible interpretations for this sentence.

> **CLEAR** Roger told Samarjit, "You are being transferred to Montreal."

> **CLEAR** Roger told Samarjit, "I am being transferred to Montreal."

Another kind of unclear pronoun reference occurs when there are too many intervening words between a pronoun and its antecedent.

> **CONFUSING** Economic recessions are the result of a multitude of factors that, in isolation, may be harmless; it is the confluence of these factors that triggers *them*.

A reader of this passage would have difficulty making the connection between the pronoun *them* and its antecedent *recessions*. To clarify, you could eliminate the pronoun by combining the two clauses.

> **CLEAR** Economic recessions are triggered by a confluence of factors that, in isolation, may be harmless.

The use of *it, this, that,* or *which* as a pronoun reference is another source of potential confusion. The problem arises when these pronouns are used to refer to whole sentences or ideas rather than to specific antecedents.

> **VAGUE** Each year during the holiday season, hundreds of bikers organize a drive to collect toys for disadvantaged children. They deposit the toys at a local donation centre on December 15. *This* is an unexpected and pleasing phenomenon.

In the preceding example, it is not clear what *This* refers to—the organized toy drive, the depositing of the toys at the donation centre, or perhaps both activities. To avoid confusion, you could revise so that *This* is eliminated.

CLEAR — Each year during the holiday season, hundreds of bikers organize a drive to collect toys for disadvantaged children. They deposit the toys at a local donation centre on December 15. The bikers' *charitable undertaking* is an unexpected and pleasing phenomenon.

39-b Misplaced Modifiers

A misplaced modifier is a word, phrase, or clause that does not point clearly to the word or words it is intended to modify.

MISPLACED — Violence is a growing problem in modern society, *which stems from fear and ignorance.*

In the preceding example, the dependent clause *which stems from fear and ignorance* follows *society* and therefore appears to modify it. It seems evident the writer intended the clause to modify *violence.*

REVISED — Violence, *which stems from fear and ignorance,* is a growing problem in modern society.

In general, a modifier should be placed either right before or right after the word or words it modifies.

Limiting modifiers, such as *only, even, exactly, almost, nearly, hardly,* and *just,* should be placed right before the words they modify. Note how changing the position of the limiting modifier alters the meaning of each of the following examples.

Only Ann Marie will receive $200 from her aunt.

Ann Marie will receive *only* $200 from her aunt.

Ann Marie will receive $200 from her *only* aunt.

A *squinting modifier* is a modifier that could refer to either the word(s) before it or the word(s) after it.

| SQUINTING | Sonny said *in the morning* he would look for the missing dog. |

You could avoid such ambiguity by revising the sentence in either of the following ways.

| REVISED | *In the morning,* Sonny said he would look for the missing dog. |

| REVISED | Sonny said he would look for the missing dog *in the morning.* |

39-c Dangling Modifiers

Dangling modifiers are words, phrases, or clauses that refer to something that is absent from the sentence. Frequently positioned at the beginnings of sentences, they appear to modify words they were never intended to modify. To revise a dangling modifier, you need to name the actor to which it properly refers.

| DANGLING | After setting out on the trail to the mountain peak, fog rolled into the valley. [Fog can't hike.] |

| REVISED | After we set out on the trail to the mountain peak, fog rolled into the valley. |

PASSIVE VOICE AND DANGLING MODIFIERS

In the active voice, the agent of the action is also the subject. In the passive voice, the object acted upon becomes the subject. The following example illustrates how a dangling modifier can result from use of the passive voice.

PASSIVE/
DANGLING   Having lost patience,

┌────── SUBJECT ──────┐
the malfunctioning computer

┌─ VERB ─┐
was replaced.

Restoring the agent of the action and re-establishing the correct relationship between subject and action removes the dangling element.

┌SUBJECT┐ ┌VERB┐

ACTIVE   Having lost patience, the student replaced

┌──── OBJECT ────┐
the malfunctioning computer.

For more information about the passive voice, see section 23-c and Chapter 46.

39-d Faulty Parallel Structure

When Shakespeare has Hamlet say "*To die, to sleep, to sleep, /* perchance *to dream*" (3.1.64–65), he is using parallel structure. Parallelism refers to a series of like grammatical elements—words, phrases, or clauses—that are expressed in repeating grammatical constructions.

WORDS   *Running, walking,* and *cycling* are all good forms of exercise.

PHRASES   To get to the market, you walk *across the street, through the park,* and *into the square.*

CLAUSES   To run for office, *you may have to join a party;* to join a party, *you may have to modify your controversial views.* [This example also includes parallel phrases—*to run for office, to join a party.*]

You violate parallel structure when you fail to use the same grammatical form for elements in a series.

NON-PARALLEL   An effective leader is capable of *inspiring* loyalty, *taking* risks, and the *acceptance* of responsibility.

PARALLEL   An effective leader is capable of *inspiring* loyalty, *taking* risks, and *accepting* responsibility.

For more information about parallel structure, see 33-c.

PART IX

Usage and Diction

40 DICTION (WORD CHOICE)

40-a Redundancy and Wordiness

A wordy sentence is one that contains more words than are necessary to convey the meaning of the sentence. For example, a sentence may contain a nonessential phrase, such as *In my opinion*, or a redundant phrase, such as *at the present time* (when *now* would suffice). To achieve precision and economy in your writing, eliminate redundant and unnecessary words and phrases.

> WORDY   It is a known fact that certain fans of rap stars, people who have devoted hundreds and hundreds of hours to learning everything possible about their idols, the stars they revere, make that the centre of their life and neglect everything else they might do or study.

> REVISED   Obsessed rap-star fans make their idols the centre of their lives.

Combining sentence elements is one of the means by which you can achieve economy in your writing (see 29-a). A process that can help you identify redundancies is the proofreading sweep (see 5-d).

40-b Appropriate Connotations

Denotation is the exact, literal meaning of a word—the kind of meaning expressed in a dictionary definition. *Connotation* refers to the values and associations attached to a word. For example, the word *home* denotes "physical structure within which one lives" and connotes such things as "refuge," "sanctuary," "haven," or "family." The connotations you select will depend on your context—specifically, your audience, purpose, and subject.

Our new line of swimwear is ideal for ~~overweight~~ full-figured customers. [A retailer would not use the word *overweight* because it connotes obesity.]

40-c Language Levels

Like speech, writing can be formal or informal. There are clear distinctions between these two language levels. For example, *employer* and *They became angry* are formal; *boss* and *They got mad* are informal. The following statements about free trade provide a further illustration of the two language levels.

INFORMAL   Free trade is just a bunch of big shots who plan to get rich at our expense.

FORMAL   Free trade is one of the mechanisms by which powerful corporate interests exploit workers for personal gain.

The language level you use will depend on your purpose, audience, and subject. More personal than formal writing, informal writing is appropriate when your objective is to please or entertain (as in the case of a personal e-mail or letter). A greater degree of formality is appropriate for academic, business, and professional writing (reports, essays, and the like).

40-d Specific and Concrete Diction

Much of the cumulative effect of your diction has to do with the extent to which you choose words that are (1) specific rather than general and (2) concrete rather than abstract. *General* words identify a class of things (*book*); *specific* words name a particular member of the class (*Sweet Tooth*). *Abstract* terms are words or phrases that refer to ideas or qualities (*justice, beauty*); *concrete* terms are words or phrases referring to things that exist in the material world (*court, painting*). Although general and abstract words are sometimes necessary to convey your meaning, specific and concrete words are usually preferable because they make your prose more vivid and precise.

GENERAL	LESS GENERAL	SPECIFIC	MORE SPECIFIC
car	Japanese car	Subaru	Subaru Forester
tree	deciduous tree	willow	weeping willow
furniture	chair	armchair	recliner

ABSTRACT	LESS ABSTRACT	CONCRETE	MORE CONCRETE
entertainment	visual entertainment	film	horror film
thoroughfare	route	street	Portage Avenue
covering	cloth protection	jacket	brown leather jacket

Wherever you have a choice, use the specific and concrete word instead of the general and abstract alternative. If you are still uncertain about the difference, examine the list above.

40-e Clichés

Clichés are expressions that were once fresh but have become tired and predictable through overuse. Here are some examples:

Raw hamburger is something you should avoid *like the plague*.

The mayor's comments are nothing but *smoke and mirrors*.

We should *leave no stone unturned* in our search for truth.

If a cliché offers an efficient way of expressing something, do not be afraid to use it. Expressions such as *tongue in cheek* and *rule of thumb* are probably preferable to unwieldy, invented alternatives. Generally, however, you should use your proofreading sweep as an opportunity to replace clichés with original and exact phrasing.

40-f Jargon

The *Concise Oxford Dictionary*'s definition of jargon may make you appreciate why you should avoid it: "Words or expressions used by a particular group or profession; barbarous or debased language; gibberish."* Although the last two definitions are warnings, the first is the one that needs closer scrutiny. Sports, academic disciplines, business, government, the arts, and many professions build up specialized vocabularies. The problem occurs when members of a group using jargon try to communicate with people not familiar with that specialized usage. Communication breaks down almost immediately.

The computer industry, with its love of acronyms and initialisms, is particularly remote from the common language. How would you fare if someone used the following terms in writing or speaking to you?

Canadian Oxford Dictionary, 2e, edited by Katherine Barber (2004). Definition.

- USB
- HTML
- DNS
- LAN
- FTP
- ISP
- RAM
- MP3
- VPN

Use specialized language only if you are sure your audience will understand it. If you must use jargon in communicating with a non-specialist audience, be sure to provide the necessary definitions.

40-g Idioms

Idioms, the peculiar expressions that every language adopts, often dictate which prepositions are used with which verbs. Here are some examples:

abide *by* (a decision)	in accordance *with*
abide *in* (a place or state)	independent *of*
according *to*	inferior *to*
accuse *of*	intend *to*
angry *with*	jealous *of*
averse *to*	preferable *to*
capable *of*	prior *to*
comply *with*	run *off* (not *off of*)
die *of*	superior *to*
different *from*	sure *of*
identical *with/to*	try *to*

ESL Focus   PREPOSITIONS USED TO INDICATE TIME AND PLACE

The following list demonstrates how to use *in*, *at*, and *on* to indicate time and place.

TO INDICATE TIME

IN   *Portion of time:* in the afternoon, in thirty seconds, in ten minutes, in two hours, in three days, in a month, in a year, in 1867, in January, in the spring

AT   *Specific time:* at 8:35, at noon, at lunch, at the start of the game

ON   *Specific day:* on Monday, on my birthday, on July 1, on St. Patrick's Day

continued

TO INDICATE PLACE

IN   *Enclosed area:* in the box, in the shower, in the living room, in the tunnel

     Location: in the street, in Hamilton, in Ontario, in Canada

AT   *Location:* at the corner, at the store, at the studio, at the computer, at the table

ON   *Surface:* on the page, on the book, on the table, on Yonge Street, on the prairies

ESL Focus   PHRASAL VERBS

A special type of idiom is the phrasal verb, which consists of a verb followed by one or two prepositions (called *particles* in this context). One of the difficulties of phrasal verbs for ESL learners is that their meaning as a unit is distinct from the meaning of the parts considered individually. The meaning of *look out* in "Look out for falling debris" (where *look out* is a phrasal verb) is different from the meaning of *look out* in "Look out the window" (where *look* and *out* are two independent words).

The following list of phrasal verbs does two things. First, it shows what preposition or adverb goes with the verb to make the phrasal verb. Second, it uses an intervening pronoun to demonstrate whether a word may come between the verb and its particle—as in *take (her/it) out.*

ask (her) out	clean up	get along
break (it) down	come across	get away
	cut (it) up	get up
bring (her/it) out	do (it) over	give (it) away
	drop (her/it) off	give in
burn (it) down/up		give up
	drop in	go out
call (her) up	drop out	go over
call (it) off	fill (it) out	grow up
clean (it) up	fill (it) up	hand (it) in

continued

hand (it) out	put (it) away	take (it) off
hang (it) up	put (it) back	take (it) over
hang on	put (it) off	take care of
help (her) out	put (it) on	think (it) over
help out	put (it) out	throw (it)
keep on	put (it)	away
keep up	together	throw (it) out
leave (it) out	put up	try (it) on
look (it) over	quiet down	try (it) out
look (it) up	run across	turn (it) down
look into	run into	turn (it) on
make (it) up	run out	turn out
pick (it) out	shut (it) off	turn up
pick (it/her)	speak up	wake (her) up
up	stay away	wake up
play around	stay up	wear out
point (it) out	take (her/it)	wrap (it) up
put (it) aside	out	

PRONOUN CASE 41

Pronoun case refers to the form of a pronoun that indicates the pronoun's function in a sentence. There are three cases in English: the *subjective* case, which is used for the subject of the sentence; the *objective* case, which is used for the object of the sentence or object of a preposition; and the *possessive* case, which indicates ownership. The pronoun forms for each of the three cases are listed below.

SUBJECTIVE CASE	OBJECTIVE CASE	POSSESSIVE CASE	
		AS AN ADJECTIVE	AS A NOUN
I	me	my	mine
we	us	our	ours
you	you	your	yours
he, she	him, her	his, her	his, hers
it, one	it, one	its, one's	its, one's
they	them	their	theirs

Seven common problems writers have in dealing with pronoun case are discussed below.

41-a *I* or *Me*

Some writers have difficulty deciding whether to use *I* or *me* in a sentence. You can avoid confusion by remembering that *I* functions as a subject, while *me* functions as an object of a verb or preposition.

SUBJECT	*I* like the mild winters in Vancouver.
OBJECT OF VERB	The mild winters in Vancouver surprised *me*.
OBJECT OF PREPOSITION	The mild winters in Vancouver appealed to *me*.

41-b Appositives

A pronoun that is used as an appositive (see 24-c) appears in the same case as the noun it renames.

>   *I*
> Two contestants, Ellen and ~~me~~, arrived early. [The appositive *Ellen and I* renames the subject *contestants*.]

> The organizers congratulated the victorious teammates, Will, Diego,
>
>   me
> and ~~I~~. [The appositive *Will, Diego, and me* renames the direct object *teammates*.]

41-c *We* or *Us*

When the pronouns *we* or *us* are used with a noun, their case depends on whether they function as a subject or an object.

>   We
> ~~Us~~ Manitobans are proud of our ethnically diverse culture. [*Manitobans* is the subject.]

us
Parks Canada rewarded ~~we~~ volunteers with a trip to Pukaskwa National Park. [*Volunteers* is the object of the verb.]

41-d Pronouns with *Than* or *As*

Using pronouns in comparisons beginning with *than* or *as* can be tricky. By mentally completing the sentence, you can determine which pronoun is appropriate.

I
Fazil is taller than ~~me~~.

him
The voters distrusted no other politician as much as ~~he~~.

Changing the pronoun case in comparisons with *than* or *as* radically alters the meaning of the sentence.

SUBJECTIVE CASE	Jean-Paul loves Maria more than *I*. [Jean-Paul loves Maria more than I do.]
OBJECTIVE CASE	Jean-Paul loves Maria more than *me*. [Jean-Paul loves Maria more than he loves me.]

41-e Pronouns with Infinitives

Pronouns that act as the subject or object of an infinitive (the base form of the verb preceded by *to*) must appear in the objective case.

SUBJECT OF INFINITIVE	He wanted *me* to see the play.
OBJECT OF INFINITIVE	He wanted to take *me* to the play.

41-f Pronouns with Gerunds and Present Participles

When pronouns modify gerunds (verbals ending in *-ing* that act as nouns) or gerund phrases, they use the possessive case.

his
I envied ~~him~~ travelling to Spain. [His modifies the gerund *travelling*.]

For more information about gerunds and other verbals, see 24-b and the ESL Focus entitled "Gerunds and Infinitives after Verbs" in 23-c.

41-g Pronouns as Subject Complements

Pronouns that function as subject complements—words that follow linking verbs (see 23-c)—always appear in the subjective case.

The people most interested in spelunking are Jordan

I
and ~~me~~.

42 PRONOUN CHOICE

42-a *Who* or *Whom*

Like *I* and *me, who* and *whom* often cause problems for writers. In formal written English, the grammatical rule is straightforward. Use *who* (or *whoever*) when the pronoun is a subject or a subject complement. Use *whom* (or *whomever*) when the pronoun is the direct or indirect object of a verb or the object of a preposition.

The man *who* had been arrested called his lawyer. [relative pronoun as subject of the clause *who had been arrested*]

The foundation grants scholarships to *whomever* it wants. [relative pronoun as object of the preposition *to*]

Who won the lacrosse game last night? [interrogative pronoun as subject]

Whom did she meet in Yellowknife? [interrogative pronoun as object]

42-b *That* or *Which*

That and *which* as relative pronouns introduce adjective clauses. Adjective clauses modify nouns or pronouns and may be restrictive or nonrestrictive. *That* is used to introduce a restrictive, or essential, clause. A restrictive clause limits the meaning of the noun it modifies and is essential to the meaning of the sentence.

Which is used to introduce a nonrestrictive, or nonessential, clause. A nonrestrictive clause, which is always set off by commas, merely adds information and therefore can be removed without changing the basic meaning of the sentence. (For more information about restrictive and nonrestrictive elements, see 48-b.)

RESTRICTIVE CLAUSE	The building *that* first caught my eye was the CN Tower.
NONRESTRICTIVE CLAUSE	Metal roofing, *which* is lightweight and inexpensive, is not suitable for this climate.

COLLECTIVE NOUNS 43

Some collective nouns, such as *linen, china, silver, hair, straw, timber, trout, fish, salmon, sheep,* and *grouse,* have identical singular and plural forms. The singular or plural nature of these collective nouns is determined by the number of the verb or pronoun that follows.

SINGULAR	The *trout jumps* high in the air, waving *its* tail as it *arches* its back.
PLURAL	Trout *are* not hard to catch on the Dean River if you know which parts of the river *they* tend to inhabit.

For more information about collective nouns and agreement, see 38-a and 38-c.

Without intending to, writers can offend members of their audience because of language choices. This fact led the APA to devote seven pages of the sixth edition of the *Publication Manual* to a discussion of how to avoid unintentional offence and ensure that language use is inclusive and unbiased.

Some of the choices we make have unintended effects. If we write "a nurse may take post-degree training to improve her employment chances," or "a doctor today finds himself forced to take additional courses on pharmaceutical developments in his specialty," we may offend male nurses and female doctors by excluding them. In cases like these, where a singular noun is necessarily followed by a singular pronoun, we create an unnecessary problem. Simply use a plural noun in this context. Any pronoun that follows will be neutral in gender, as with *they* or *their*. Our statement now reads "nurses may take post-degree training to improve their employment chances." On other occasions, we might avoid offence by using a specific rather than a general descriptor, as in "people between 75 and 90" rather than "old people." Whenever you encounter a situation where using a singular pronoun or a general descriptor may give offence, try replacing that usage with one that is inclusive.

You will find the same challenge when you are dealing with ethnic or racial descriptions. Generally, you can use a more specific or more general descriptor to avoid offending any of your readers. However, there are complexities involved in respecting the ethnicity/nationality of other people. In "Review Article: The Incredible Vagueness of Being British/English," Robin Cohen observes that "one can be Muslim in the Mosque, Asian in the street, Asian British at political hustings and British when travelling abroad, all in a single day."[1]

At one time, we used *Indo-Canadian* to describe a particular nationality, but that usage is shifting to *South Asian*. The problem in this case is that the new choice is so general that your reference is equally general. If you are writing about the Diwali festival, *Indo-Canadian* might be a better choice. You will also find many instances of hyphenated Canadians: German-Canadians, Dutch-Canadians, Filipino-Canadians, Chinese-Canadians, and so on. There are many Canadians who don't wish to be described as a

---

[1] Robin Cohen, "Review Article: The Incredible Vagueness of Being British/English," *International Affairs* 76, no. 3 (2000): 582.

hyphenated Canadian, and we may be moving towards the American and British usage of non-hyphenated constructions. Interestingly, the Americans have preferred unhyphenated versions such as Asian Americans, Hispanic Americans, and Polish Americans for a long time. You should feel free to use the unhyphenated version if you prefer it.

American usage also differs from Canadian in dealing with native Americans. They generally choose among three alternatives: Native Americans, Native North Americans, and Indians. In Canada, the majority choice is *First Nations people* for Aboriginal persons who are not Inuit or Métis. It is sometimes possible to identify people more specifically, as Haida, Cree, and so on; however, the term *First Nations* remains the dominant one. *Aboriginal* or *Indigenous* are often used when referring to First Nations, Inuit, and Métis as a group. Again, the intention in all these cases is to move away from names that may offend and towards inclusive names.

In cases involving sexual orientation, usage is evolving with the same intention: to be inclusive and unbiased in our practices. This often means multiplying the terms we once had and being more exact. Where we once might have limited ourselves to *heterosexual* and *homosexual*, we have introduced an expanded number of descriptors. The word *orientation* is in general use, with additional words to describe the person's orientation more exactly. So we have *heterosexual orientation*, *gay and lesbian orientation* (*gay* is sometimes applied to both men and women), *transgendered orientation*, and *bisexual orientation*. The terms are evolving, and we will no doubt see more refinement, with *orientation* being the key word in the evolving descriptors. The use of *homosexual* is disappearing because of its lack of precision. The abbreviation *LGBT* (for lesbian, gay, bisexual, and transsexual) is more commonly heard.

When discussing students in their earlier years, usage has also changed. Where we might once have talked about an overactive student or a student with difficulty concentrating, we now use terms we find in the daily newspaper such as ADD (Attention Deficit Disorder), ADHD (Attention Deficit Hyperactive Disorder), Autism, Differential Learning Abilities, Special Needs children, and a growing list of other terms.

A person's age can be expressed in a more inclusive style than simply talking about young people and old people. *Adolescent* may be used for one group, *young* for another, then *middle-aged*, and *seniors* or *elders*. If you are using a specific age group in your analysis, or even multiple-age groups, it is best to state their age range in specific terms: for example, people aged 30 to 45, people aged 50 to 65, and people aged 65 to 80. You also want to be as inclusive as possible in referring to age and the challenges that go along with it. We no longer see people being referred to as senile, for instance. We are more likely to read a piece on the difficulties associated with different forms of dementia or how dementia may be challenged and slowed down.

In simple terms, therefore, there are many ways in which we can cultivate inclusive language when writing about people of different ages, ethnicities, genders, racial and ethnic groups, and sexual orientation. In each case, we should cultivate language that is inclusive and free from bias, whether explicit or implied. We must extend to all people the respect we want for ourselves.

The seventh edition of the *MLA Handbook for Writers of Research Papers* has an excellent list of materials for ensuring our writing uses inclusive language. Its Appendix A.3: Guides to Non-Discriminatory Language (259–260) lists twelve reference books, including three dictionaries of inclusive language choices. If you have further questions, consult this list.

The sixth edition of the *Publication Manual of the American Psychological Association* has a section entitled "Reducing Bias in Language" (70–77), which provides useful advice on how to recognize language that could offend and specific points on how to ensure unbiased language is used in your writing. The manual also provides a reference on p. 71 to the Guidelines for Unbiased Language on the APA Style website: www.apastyle.org.

COMPARATIVES AND SUPERLATIVES

45

All adjectives and adverbs have a positive or base form (*hard, slowly*). In addition to their positive form, most adjectives and adverbs have a comparative form (*harder, more slowly*) and a superlative form (*hardest, most slowly*). The comparative form is used to compare two things, while the superlative form is used to compare three or more things.

COMPARATIVE	Alberta is a *larger* province than Nova Scotia.
SUPERLATIVE	Quebec is the *largest* province in Canada.

45-a Irregular Comparatives and Superlatives

Not all adjectives and adverbs follow a standard pattern when it comes to the formation of comparatives and

POSITIVE	COMPARATIVE	SUPERLATIVE
good	better	best
well	better	best
bad	worse	worst
badly	worse	worst
many	more	most
much	more	most
some	more	most
little	less	least
far	farther/further	farthest/furthest

superlatives. The three forms of some of these atypical adjectives and adverbs are listed below.

45-b Absolute Terms

Absolute terms, such as *equal, fatal, perfect, square,* and *unique,* should not be given a comparative or superlative form. You cannot describe something as *more unique* or *most unique,* for example, because there cannot be degrees of uniqueness.

The skiing conditions couldn't be ~~more perfect~~. *better*

Is arsenic more ~~fatal~~ than strychnine? *deadly*

The CN Tower is the most ~~unique~~ building in Toronto. *unusual*

46 ACTIVE AND PASSIVE VOICE

The voice of a verb depends on whether the subject of the sentence is acting or being acted upon. In the active voice, the subject *does* the action; in the passive voice, the subject *receives* the action.

ACTIVE The Governor General *dissolved* Parliament.

PASSIVE Parliament *was dissolved* by the Governor General.

Writers are generally advised to use the active voice as much as possible because it results in prose that is not only crisper and clearer but also more dynamic.

The use of the passive voice is appropriate if the doer of the action is unknown or less important than the recipient of the action.

In 1918, Canadian women, after spirited protest, *were given* the right to vote in federal elections. [doer less important than recipient]

For more on active and passive voice, see 23-c and 39-c.

47 SPLIT INFINITIVES

An infinitive consists of the base form of a verb preceded by *to* (*to walk, to believe, to represent*). A split infinitive occurs when the two parts of the infinitive are separated by a modifier consisting of a word, phrase, or clause (*to fervently believe*). A split infinitive that is awkward or potentially confusing to the reader should be eliminated.

AWKWARD The defendant wants *to* as soon as possible *appeal* the guilty verdict.

REVISED The defendant wants *to appeal* the guilty verdict as soon as possible.

Punctuation

Comma usage falls into two major divisions: commas used to *separate* and commas used to *set off.*

48-a Commas to Separate

1. Use a comma before a coordinating conjunction (*and, but, yet, so, or, nor, for*) joining independent clauses.

> Canadian history is replete with examples of
>
> federal–provincial conflict, so the wrangling
> ^
> about transfer payments is hardly
>
> surprising.

2. Use commas to separate three or more items—words, phrases, or clauses—in a series.

> Carrots, beets, turnips, and potatoes were
> ^   ^   ^
> common winter vegetables in nineteenth-
>
> century Canada.

> Crosby swept across the blue line, pivoted
> ^
> around the defenceman, and barged into the
> ^
> slot.

Although some writers prefer to omit the comma separating the last two items, most authorities recommend that this final comma—called a *series* or *serial comma*—be retained to avoid confusion.

3. Use commas with dates, addresses, and titles. Note the absence of the comma before the postal code in the address example.

> Send the parcel to 2345 Willowbrook
>
> Crescent, Langley, British Columbia
> ^   ^
> V3B 2K4.

NOTE: The newer date style of having the day precede the month removes the need for a comma, as in 28 June 2014.

48-b Commas to Set Off

1. Use commas to set off introductory elements.

   Unfortunately, many born politicians never
   enter politics. [adverb]

   The vocalist is hopeless; *however*, the new
   dancer shows promise. [conjunctive adverb]

   Before the election, the candidates promised
   more than they could ever hope to deliver.
   [prepositional phrase]

   Marsha having arrived, we began the meeting.
   [absolute phrase]

2. Use commas to set off nonrestrictive elements.
   An element is nonrestrictive if it adds information not essential to the meaning of the sentence;
   an element is restrictive if it defines or limits the
   noun in a way that is essential to the meaning of
   the sentence. (For more information about
   restrictive and nonrestrictive elements, see 42-b.)

   The 2006 film *Bon Cop, Bad Cop, which
   grossed more than any previous Canadian
   film*, was advertised as the first truly
   bilingual English-French film made in
   Canada. [nonrestrictive adjective clause]

   RSPs, *despite their risks*, remain the
   bedrock of retirement planning for many
   Canadians. [nonrestrictive prepositional phrase]

3. Use commas to set off transitional expressions,
   parenthetical expressions, explanatory terms, and
   contrasted elements.

   Whole wheat and vegetable oils, *for example*,
   are rich in vitamin E. [transitional expression]

A cerebrovascular incident, *or stroke,* is a sudden stoppage of blood flow to a portion of the brain. [explanatory term]

4. Use commas to set off forms of direct address, interrogative tags, the words *yes* and *no,* and interjections.

Ladies and gentlemen, kindly take your seats. [direct address]

You liked the film, *didn't you*? [interrogative tag]

Oh, I wouldn't go that far. [interjection]

COMMAS TO SEPARATE
1. before a coordinating conjunction joining independent clauses
2. words, phrases, or clauses in a series
3. with dates, addresses, and titles

COMMAS TO SET OFF
1. introductory elements
2. nonrestrictive elements
3. transitional expressions, parenthetical expressions, explanatory terms, and contrasted elements
4. direct address, interrogative tags, the words *yes* and *no,* and interjections

---

48-c Misuses of the Comma

Do *not* use a comma in the following situations.

1. To set off restrictive elements

The newspaper's entertainment reporter is interviewing the singer/ *Alicia Keys.*

2. Between a subject and a verb or a verb and an object (when there are no intervening phrases)

The governor of the Bank of Canada observed/ that the high value of the Canadian dollar/ has caused problems for Canadian exports in the United States.

3. After the last item in a series

> Political parties are always looking for talented, articulate, and ambitious/ people to run for office.

4. Between cumulative adjectives

> He is a dear/ old/ man.

5. Before or after a coordinating conjunction joining elements other than clauses.

> She worked for a newspaper/ and trained as a lawyer before entering politics.

6. With a question mark or an exclamation mark

> "Watch out!"/ James shouted.

THE SEMICOLON 49

1. Use a semicolon to link closely related independent clauses.

> The magazine article is not based on facts; it
> is based on rumour and speculation.
>   ^

2. Use semicolons to separate items in a series when one or more of the items has internal punctuation.

> The unlikely high school clique consists of
> Mai, who loves to party; Samantha, who loves
>   ^
> to study; and Dave, who loves to sleep.
>   ^

THE COLON 50

1. Use a colon after an independent clause to introduce a *list*, a *quotation*, an *appositive*, or an *explanation*.

Visitors to foreign countries require the following: a foreign-language phrase book, a viable bank card, health insurance, and a desire to experience different cultures. [list]

The coach urged his struggling team to reflect on the immortal words of Yogi Berra: "It ain't over till it's over." [quotation]

2. Use a colon with the following: hours, minutes, and seconds; salutations, attention/subject lines, and copy notations in letters; elements in memo headings; titles and subtitles; biblical chapters and verses; and parts of bibliographical entries.

HOURS, MINUTES, AND SECONDS

He crossed the finish line at 10:34:23.

SALUTATIONS IN LETTERS

Dear Sir or Madam:

ATTENTION/SUBJECT LINES IN LETTERS

Attention: Kulwinder Singh

Subject: Board of directors meeting

COPY NOTATIONS IN LETTERS

cc: Thomas Ruffini

ELEMENTS IN MEMO HEADINGS

To: Sylvie Campeau

From: Heather Thomas

Date: April 2, 2014

Subject: Year-end report

TITLES AND SUBTITLES

Shadow Maker: The Life of Gwendolyn MacEwen

BIBLICAL CHAPTERS AND VERSES

Matthew 6:28

PARTS OF BIBLIOGRAPHICAL ENTRIES

Page, P. K. *Up on the Roof*. Erin, ON: Porcupine's Quill, 2007. [The colon separates the place of publication from the publisher.]

QUOTATION MARKS 51

51-a Direct Speech

1. Place double quotation marks around direct speech. Do not use quotation marks for *indirect speech,* speech that is reported or paraphrased rather than quoted directly.

   > Northrop Frye once observed, "If a sculptor were to make a statue of a patriotic Canadian, he would depict somebody holding his breath and crossing his fingers." [direct speech]

   > She said she would meet us at the restaurant. [indirect speech]

2. Use commas to set off speaker tags from quotations.

   > "The true character of the historical Grace Marks," writes Atwood, "remains an enigma."

   EXCEPTION: Omit the comma when the speaker tag follows a quotation that ends with a question mark or an exclamation mark.

   > "Are you ready to go?" he asked.

3. Use single quotation marks to enclose quotations within quotations.

   > Alan Hustak's book *Titanic: The Canadian Story* tells of a British passenger, a woman named Esther Hart, who had a

premonition of disaster. As Hart's daughter later recalled, "When she saw a headline in a newspaper that their new ship was unsinkable, she said, 'Now I know why I am frightened. This is flying in the face of God.'"

51-b Short and Long Quotations

1. Use quotation marks to enclose a prose quotation of four or fewer typed lines (MLA style), forty words (APA style), or eight lines/one hundred words (Chicago style) in your essay.

    > Carol Shields has characterized Susanna Moodie, that most reluctant of Canada's early pioneers, as "a Crusoe baffled by her own heated imagination, the dislocated immigrant who never fully accepts or rejects her adopted country."

    When the prose quotation runs longer than four typed lines (MLA), forty words (APA), or six to eight lines/one hundred words (Chicago), set it off from the text by indenting one inch (2.5 cm) (MLA), one tab (Chicago), or five spaces (APA) from the left margin. A quotation presented in this format, called a *block quotation,* is not enclosed in quotation marks. It is double-spaced (MLA, APA, and Chicago).

    > In *The Great Lone Land,* William Francis Butler captures the immensity of the Canadian prairie and the damage that Europeans did to it as they moved west across the country:
    >
    > > Hundreds of thousands of skeletons dot the short scant grass; and when fire had laid barer still the level surface, the bleached ribs and skulls of long-killed bison whiten far and near

the dark burnt prairie. There is

something unspeakably melancholy in

the aspect of this portion of the

Northwest. [MLA style]

2. Use quotation marks to enclose a poetry quotation that runs no more than three lines. Note the use of slashes to indicate the separation of lines (see Chapter 53).

In "Cypresses," D. H. Lawrence writes, "Evil, what is evil? / There is only one evil, to deny life."

A poetry quotation longer than three lines is set off line by line as a block quotation.

The opening lines of "A Poison Tree"

illustrate the deceptive simplicity of William

Blake's language:

I was angry with my friend:

I told my wrath, my wrath did end.

I was angry with my foe:

I told it not, my wrath did grow.

51-c Titles

Use quotation marks to enclose the titles of essays and articles, short stories, poems, songs, speeches, parts of books, and episodes of radio and television programs.

An article entitled "Answering Systems from Hell" captures people's frustrations with corporate and governmental phone-answering trees. [article]

A similar note of melancholy is struck in Alice Munro's story "Jakarta." [short story]

My favourite Barenaked Ladies song is "If I Had $1000000." [song]

The authors of this computer guide discuss everything from mice to modems in a chapter entitled "Inside Out." [part of a book]

In the episode "The Wolf and the Lion" in *Game of Thrones*, season one, Tyrion Lannister is kept as a prisoner at the vale in the terrifying sky cells.

NOTE: Italicize the titles of complete works, such as books and periodicals (see 58-a).

51-d Other Uses for Quotation Marks

1. Quotation marks are sometimes used to set off words used ironically.

   My "assets" consist of an Ikea bedroom suite and an overdrawn bank account.

2. Quotation marks may be used to enclose words used as words or terms.

   The plural of "datum" is "data."

   NOTE: Italics may be used instead of quotation marks for this purpose (see 58-b).

3. Use quotation marks for words coined (invented) by a writer.

   Interviews with "sexperts" are the backbone of Miller's irreverent study of sexual etiquette.

51-e Quotation Marks with Other Punctuation

1. Place commas and periods *inside* closing quotation marks.

   "I'm studying for the chemistry exam," said Ahmed. "I expect to be up all night."

2. Place colons and semicolons *outside* quotation marks.

   Here is the terrible truth about the "anorexia industry": it reinforces the very phenomenon it is designed to combat.

3. Put question marks and exclamation marks inside quotation marks if they belong to the quo-

tation and outside if they apply to the sentence as a whole.

> He said, "What's the matter?"

> Has anyone read John Ralston Saul's essay "The Politics of Common Sense"?

4. Place footnote numbers and page citations outside quotation marks.

> As Abraham Maslow comments in his book *Motivation and Personality*, "It is quite true that man lives by bread alone when there is no bread."[1]

> In *The Intelligence of Dogs*, Stanley Coren describes the Dandie Dinmont terrier as "a very distinctive little dog with deep soulful eyes" (13).

THE APOSTROPHE 52

The apostrophe has three main uses: to indicate the possessive case; to substitute for letters in contractions; and to form the plural of letters, numbers, and words used as words or terms.

52-a Possession

1. Add an apostrophe and -*s* (-*'s*) to form the possessive case of singular nouns (including those ending in -*s*) and indefinite pronouns.

> The *witness's* testimony is full of contradictions.

> It could have been *anyone's* book.

2. Add an apostrophe to form the possessive case of plural nouns ending in -*s*. If the plural does not end in -*s*, add an apostrophe and -*s*.

> The *Joneses'* house has been sold.

> We are raising money for the *children's* fund.

3. To indicate joint possession by two or more owners, make only the last noun possessive. To indicate individual possession, make all nouns possessive.

> *Nova and Seb's* presentation was the most polished.

> *Candace's* and *Todd's* political views differ greatly.

4. To form the possessive of compound nouns (a noun consisting of two or more words), add an apostrophe and *-s* to the last word.

> *Joan of Arc's* battles against the English helped to revive French patriotism.

FORMING THE POSSESSIVE CASE WITH APOSTROPHES

Singular noun not ending in *-s*	add -'s
Singular noun ending in *-s*	add -'s
Indefinite pronoun	add -'s
Plural noun ending in *-s*	add apostrophe
Plural noun not ending in *-s*	add -'s
Two or more nouns	
joint possession	add -'s to last noun
individual possession	add -'s to all nouns
Compound noun	add -'s to last word compound

52-b Contractions

Contractions are formed when certain letters are left out of words or phrases. As the following examples illustrate, an apostrophe is used to replace the missing letter or letters:

cannot/can't	she would, she had/she'd
does not/doesn't	there is, there has/there's
I am/I'm	you will/you'll
I would/I'd	who is/who's
it is/it's	will not/won't

Contractions are used frequently in conversation and informal writing, but they are usually avoided in formal writing.

52-c Plurals

Do not use apostrophes to form the plural of letters, numbers, and words used as words.

> At the 2002 Olympics, the judges awarded Canadian pairs skaters Salé and Pelletier *6.0s* for their signature "Love Story" program. [number]

> The two *Incompletes* on Tim's transcript were a direct result of his illness earlier that year. [word used as a word]

NOTE: Styles change, and the former trend was to use an apostrophe for many of these plurals (e.g., the three R's, the 1990's). Where there is the possibility of confusion or awkwardness, maintain the apostrophe.

THE SLASH 53

1. In a short quotation, use the slash to separate lines of a poem included within your text. Leave a space before and after each slash.

   > In "Low Tide on Grand Pre," Bliss Carman describes the aging process: "I deemed / That time was ripe, and years had done / Their wheeling underneath the sun."

2. Use a slash to separate the numerator and denominator in a fraction and the elements of an abbreviated date. Do not include a space before and after the slash in these situations.

   $$x/a + y/b = 1; \ 09/08/25$$

3. A slash is sometimes used instead of a hyphen to indicate a period overlapping two calendar years and to separate paired terms such as *student/teacher* and *producer/director*.

1. Use parentheses to enclose supplementary information.

   > Tom Thomson's evocative paintings of northern Ontario's rugged landscapes (landscapes now threatened by logging interests) have lost none of their ability to captivate.

2. The material enclosed by parentheses may, among other things, identify, amplify, illustrate, clarify, or comment.

   > A study of Ottawa politics would necessarily focus on the three Ps (power, perks, and patronage) and the major players (MPs, deputy ministers, bureaucrats, lobbyists, and the press). [identifies]

3. Parentheses are also used to enclose numbers or letters in a list.

   > To conduct the experiment, you require the following materials: (1) safety goggles, (2) electrolysis apparatus, (3) water, (4) 5 g sodium sulphate, (5) power supply, (6) electrical leads, and (7) wooden splints.

55 BRACKETS

1. Use square brackets to enclose words or comments you have inserted into a quotation.

   > Frank Newell, an embalmer from Yarmouth, "unexpectedly found [among the *Titanic*'s recovered dead] the body of a relative."

   > Timothy Findley described Glenn Gould as one of the "god-people, [who] are the truly, absolutely gifted, almost beyond human dimension or human comprehension."

The second of the preceding example sentences shows how brackets can be used to make a quotation grammatically consistent with the rest of the sentence.

2. If there is an error in the quotation, you can follow the error with a bracketed *sic*. Latin for "so" or "thus," *sic* is a way of telling readers that the mistake was in the original.

> In a press release, the CEO said the company would "do everything possible to accompany [*sic*] the strikers' demands."

1. Like commas or parentheses, dashes may be used to set off parenthetical material. Dashes bring more emphasis to the added material than either commas or parentheses.

> The biographer's account of Leonard Cohen's life—from his comfortable Westmount childhood, through his early days as a struggling poet, to his second career as a songwriter/performer—is meticulous and gracefully written.

2. Like colons, dashes may be used to introduce a list, an appositive, or an explanation.

> The alternative bookstore offers seminars on three New Age topics—holistic medicine, Gaia theory, and reincarnation. [list]

> David Cronenberg's twin passions—science and literature—are expressed in many of his films. [appositive]

3. A dash may also be used to signal an interruption or an abrupt shift in tone or thought.

> "I don't understand what—" Liz broke off in confusion. [explanation]

4. In MLA-, APA-, and Chicago-style essays, you can use either two hyphens (--) or a word-processing em dash (—) to form a dash. There is no space before or after a dash.

1. The omission of words from a quotation is indicated by the use of ellipsis points. Use three points to indicate the omission of words within a sentence or the omission of a complete sentence or more within a quotation. (To indicate an omission that is preceded by a complete sentence, use four points, the first of which functions as a sentence period.)

> In their introduction to the *ITP Nelson Canadian Dictionary of the English Language*, the authors write, "We have . . . sought to show how the development of . . . Canadian English . . . mirrors our development as a nation."

Here is the original text of the quotation in the above example (omissions in italics):

> We have *also* sought to show how the development of *our own variety of English*, Canadian English, mirrors our development as a nation.

2. Use ellipsis points when you omit material from the middle or end of a quotation.

> Ben Okri writes, "we are living the stories planted in us early or along the way, or we are . . . living the stories we planted . . . in ourselves."

Do not use ellipsis points at the beginning of a quotation.

3. When your omission follows a period, include the period and then add the ellipsis. No space appears between the last letter and the first point because that point is the period of the quoted sentence and is not part of the ellipsis.

> In 1982, pre-tax bank profits were $1630.2 million, while taxes were $104.8 million. . . . an effective tax rate of 6.4% . . ." (Calvert 39).

4. MLA style requires that you place brackets around ellipsis points you have utilized to signal an omis-

sion from a quotation if the author of the quotation has already used ellipsis points in the passage.

In "Just Rain, Racolet," Brand's narrator remarks, "So I did not mention the unnecessary clutter of tourists and cameras which had to be policed and . . . So I took this as a gift, this intimacy at Turtle Beach [. . .] and the lights and the hotel and the cigarette-smoking man Vi told to 'have a little respect.'"

5. The omission of one or more lines of poetry is indicated by a line of spaced periods running approximately the length of the preceding line.

Turning and turning in the widening gyre

The falcon cannot hear the falconer;

Things fall apart; the centre cannot hold;

. . . .

Surely some revelation is at hand;

Surely the Second Coming is at hand.*

— William Butler Yeats, "The Second Coming"

6. Ellipsis points may be used to mark a pause or hesitation.

Sergio said, "It's just . . . I mean, if you want to know the truth . . . I'm not sure what caused the accident."

---

*Excerpt from "The Second Coming" by William Butler Yeats.

Mechanics

58-a Titles of Works

In word-processed documents, titles of complete works are italicized. In handwritten work, whether on exams or in-class tests, underlining is used to indicate italics (<u>The English Patient</u>). Quotation marks are used for short poems and titles that are parts of complete works, such as essays and short stories (see 51-c).

BOOKS	*The Last Crossing*
CHOREOGRAPHIC WORKS	Balanchine's *Agon*
COMIC STRIPS	*Sherman's Lagoon*
FILMS	*There Will Be Blood*
JOURNALS	*Canadian Historical Review*
LONG MUSICAL COMPOSITIONS	Puccini's *La Bohème*
LONG POEMS	*Seed Catalogue*
MAGAZINES	*Maclean's*
NEWSPAPERS	*The Globe and Mail*
PAMPHLETS	Paine's *Common Sense*
PLAYS	*Coming Up for Air*
RADIO PROGRAMS	*Ideas*
TELEVISION PROGRAMS	*Friends*
WORKS OF VISUAL ART	Michelangelo's *David*

NOTE: Do not italicize the titles of (1) sacred books, such as the Bible, the Talmud, or the Koran; (2) legal and political documents, such as Magna Carta, the Charter of Rights and Freedoms, the Criminal Code, or the Canadian Environmental Protection Act; and (3) software, such as Microsoft Word or WordPerfect.

58-b Other Uses

1.   Italicize the names of aircraft, spacecraft, ships, and trains.

It was the flight of the space shuttle *Discovery* in 1992 that made Roberta Bondar the second Canadian astronaut in space.

NOTE: Do not use italics for vehicle types (Boeing 747, Bombardier CRJ 1000).

2. Italicize foreign words and phrases, such as *livre d'artiste*.

    NOTE: Do not italicize foreign words that are frequently used by English speakers and thus are considered part of the English language (e.g., ad infinitum, bona fide, habeas corpus, noblesse oblige, per capita, tour de force, vice versa).

3. Use italics for the biological classifications of plants, animals, insects, and microorganisms. Note that the genus name but not the species name is capitalized: *Felis domesticus*.

4. Italicize words, letters, and numbers referred to as words.

    He thought *committed* was spelled with one *m* and one *t*.

    NOTE: Quotation marks may be used instead of italics for this purpose. (See 51-d.)

5. Italicize the names of legal cases.

    Bhinder v. Canadian National Railway

CAPITALIZATION 59

59-a Sentence Capitals

1. The first word of a sentence is capitalized unless the sentence is contained within another sentence and enclosed in parentheses or dashes.

The author follows his introduction with a historical overview of the right wing in Canada (a decline in racist activity after the Second World War ended in a "virtual explosion" in the 1970s and 1980s) and detailed sections on the Canadian Nazi Party and the Edmund Burke Society.

2. A quoted complete sentence that is blended into the writer's sentence begins with a lowercase letter.

   George Orwell believed that "modern English, especially written English, is full of bad habits."

   If the quoted complete sentence has a more remote syntactic relation to the rest of the sentence, the initial capital is retained.

   As George Orwell said, "Modern English, especially written English, is full of bad habits."

3. If a quoted sentence is interrupted by a speaker tag (*he said*, *she wrote*, etc.), do not capitalize the first word after the speaker tag.

   "After one of these storms," she said, "the sky looks like pink cotton candy."

4. When two complete sentences are linked by a colon, the second sentence does not begin with a capital letter unless it is a quotation.

   The government took drastic measures: it imposed martial law.

   Jack McClelland's response to the failure of *The Stone Angel* to capture a Governor General's Award was characteristically blunt: "It's a goddamn disgrace."

   NOTE: A sentence that follows a dash always starts with a small letter: *There's no doubt about it—the honeymoon's over.*

59-b Proper Nouns

1. Proper nouns name particular persons, places, and things. Common nouns name generic classes of persons, places, and things.

PROPER NOUNS	COMMON NOUNS
Mount Logan	mountain
Giller Prize	book award

2. Capitalize all proper nouns and the adjectives derived from them. Do not capitalize common nouns unless they begin a sentence. The following categories of words are always capitalized:

- personal names
- days of the week and months of the year
- official and popular names of geographic areas
- official names of organizations
- names of deities, religions, and religious writings
- names of racial, linguistic, religious, and other groups of people
- names of civic holidays and holy days
- names of historical periods
- names of specific aircraft, spacecraft, ships, and trains
- names of structures
- names of planets, stars, and other bodies in space

3. Capitalize titles of persons that directly precede a proper name. Do not capitalize titles used alone or following a proper name.

> Prime Minister Harper first met with President Obama in 2008.

> Stephen Harper, the prime minister, first met with the U.S. president in 2008.

59-c Titles of Works

In MLA style, capitalize the first and last words in titles of works and all other words except for articles, prepositions, coordinating conjunctions, and the *to* part of an infinitive. MLA also recommends that a title for a work be italicized.

APA style requires that the first word of a title or subtitle and all proper nouns be capitalized. It also recommends that a title be italicized. Chicago style allows you to follow either the MLA or APA format in capitalizing a title but recommends that the title be italicized.

60 ABBREVIATIONS

60-a Titles of Persons

1. Academic, religious, political, and military titles are usually abbreviated when they directly precede a full name and spelled out when they precede a surname alone.

   Gov. Gen. David Johnston   Governor General Johnston

2. A title that stands alone is not abbreviated.

   professor

   My English ~~prof.~~ says that Walt Whitman is considered the greatest American poet.

3. Do not use a title before a name if another title follows the name. The title *Dr. Yetta Abramsky, Ph.D.* is redundant. Either *Dr. Yetta Abramsky* or *Yetta Abramsky, Ph.D.* would be acceptable .

60-b Geographical Names

1. The names of countries are usually spelled out in running text. A common exception is *U.S.*, which may appear in text as an adjective but not as a noun.

   UNACCEPTABLE   Canada's largest trading partner is the U.S.

   ACCEPTABLE   Many Canadians are troubled by our dependence on the U.S. economy.

2. In bibliographical citations, the names of provinces, territories, and states are abbreviated. Listed below are the traditional abbreviations for provinces/territories and the two-letter abbreviations used by Canada Post.

	TRADITIONAL	CANADA POST
Alberta	Alta.	AB
British Columbia	B.C.	BC
Manitoba	Man.	MB
New Brunswick	N.B.	NB
Newfoundland and Labrador	Nfld. and Lab.	NL
Northwest Territories	N.W.T.	NT
Nunavut	—	NU
Nova Scotia	N.S.	NS
Ontario	Ont.	ON
Prince Edward Island	P.E.I.	PE
Quebec	Que. or P.Q.	QC
Saskatchewan	Sask.	SK
Yukon Territory	Y.T.	YT

60-c Acronyms and Initialisms

1. *Acronyms* are abbreviations that can be pronounced as words (*PEN, NAFTA, RAM*). *Initialisms* are abbreviations that are pronounced letter by letter (*MP, VHS, IBM*).

2. If you think your audience is unlikely to know what an acronym or initialism stands for, write the full name at the first use, followed by the acronym or initialism in parentheses; in subsequent mentions, use the acronym or initialism by itself. If you are using an acronym or initialism only once or twice in an essay, write the full name at each mention.

3. Geographical initialisms may be written with or without periods (*U.K.* or *UK, U.S.* or *USA*).

60-d Era Designations and Time of Day

1. The abbreviation A.D. precedes a date, and B.C. follows a date. More current alternatives are B.C.E. and C.E.

1000 B.C.   before Christ

A.D. 1700   *anno Domini* (in the year of our Lord)

1000 B.C.E.   before the common era

1700 C.E.   common era

NOTE: Era designations are often set in small caps with or without periods (A.D./AD).

2. The abbreviations A.M. and P.M. are acceptable only when used with figures.

6:45 A.M.   *ante meridiem* (before noon)

10:30 P.M.   *post meridiem* (after noon)

NOTE: A.M. and P.M. are often set in lowercase letters (a.m./p.m.) or in small caps (P.M.).

61 NUMBERS

61-a Spelling Out

1. Numbers that can be expressed in one or two words should be spelled out in formal writing. (In technical and business writing, figures are often preferred, although usage varies.) Use figures for numbers that require more than two words to spell out.

894

Wayne Gretzky scored ~~eight hundred and ninety-four~~ goals in the course of his NHL career.

EXCEPTIONS: (1) Related numbers should be expressed in the same style: *Alison Redford captured sixty-one of eighty-seven seats in the 2012 Alberta federal election.* (2) To express sums of money in the millions or billions of dollars, you may use a combination of numbers and words accompanied by the dollar sign (*$15 billion*).

2. Do not begin a sentence with a figure, even when other numbers in the sentence are expressed in figures.

> Five
> ~~5~~ employees are responsible for processing between 80 and 120 application forms.

A sentence that begins with a long number can be revised to avoid awkwardness.

| UNACCEPTABLE | 175 people attended Bob and Lynn's wedding. |
| REVISED | There were 175 people at Bob and Lynn's wedding. |

61-b Punctuation of Numbers

In traditional English style, commas are used to separate groups of three digits. In SI (*Système international d'unités*) style, a space is used to mark the separation. The traditional style is appropriate for academic and general-interest materials. SI usage is usually restricted to technical or scientific writing.

85,000 [traditional]; 85 000 [SI]

NOTE: In four-digit numbers, the use of a separating comma is optional: *Mount Everest is 8863 (or 8,863) metres above sea level.*

61-c Uses of Numbers

Numbers are appropriate in the following instances:

ADDRESSES	215 Pacific Avenue, Suite 1407
DATES	August 24, 2008 (*or* 24 August 2008)
DECIMALS, FRACTIONS	0.09, 3/4
DIVISIONS OF BOOKS	Chapter 8, Volume 2, page 63
DIVISIONS OF PLAYS	Act II, Scene iv (*or* Act 2, Scene 4), lines 5–13 (*or,* in MLA style, 2.4.5-13)

EXACT SUMS OF MONEY	$4829, $2.51
SCORES	a 6–5 victory
RATIOS	a ratio of 3 to 1, 2-to-1 odds
TIME OF DAY	9:00 A.M., 2:58 P.M. (*but* four o'clock)

61-d Symbols and Units of Measurement

Symbols (such as %, ¢, =, @, and #) and units of measurement (such as *cm*, *g*, *km*, *kg*, *L*, and *m*) are appropriate in tables but not in the body of an essay, according to MLA.

In APA style, it is appropriate to use the symbol in the body of the essay, but Chicago style recommends that "percent" be written out in humanities essays unless the essay contains many references to "percent," in which case the symbol is acceptable.

EXCEPTIONS: (1) The dollar sign is always used with figures: *At the time of her death, the Toronto-born poet Gwendolyn MacEwen had a bank account balance of $2.02.* (2) Symbols may be used to express temperature (18°C, 102°F).

62 HYPHENS

62-a Compound Words

A compound word is a word made up of two or more words. Compound words occur as separate words, as single words, or with hyphens.

SEPARATE WORDS	free trade, hard disk
SINGLE WORD	makeup, grandfather, textbook, workplace
WITH HYPHENS	medium-sized, first-class, ex-wife

Following are some guidelines concerning the use of hyphens in compound words:

1. Use hyphens to connect the parts of compounds that function as adjectives (*well-known writer, six-year-old boy, large-scale project*).

2. Use a hyphen after the prefixes *all-, self-, ex-*, and *quasi-* (*all-inclusive dinner, self-appointed leader, ex-convict, quasi-scientific theory*). Do not, however, use a hyphen in the words *selfish, selfhood, selfless*, and *selfsame*.

3. Use a hyphen with prefixes that precede a capital or a figure (*non-Native, post-2000*).

4. Use hyphens to prevent readers from misunderstanding the relationship between adjectives and the words they modify. *Light blue coat*, for example, could mean either a blue coat that is light in weight or a coat that is light blue in colour. Adding a hyphen would clarify the latter meaning (*light-blue coat*).

5. Use a hyphen in spelled-out fractions and in number compounds from twenty-one to ninety-nine (*fifty-two, one-seventh*).

6. A hyphen may be used to separate paired terms (*author-critic, parent-child, French-English*). A slash is also used for this purpose. (See Chapter 53.)

7. Use a hyphen to separate identical vowels or consonants in some compounds (*anti-inflation, de-emphasize, bell-like*).

8. Use a hyphen to distinguish between such words as *recover* and *re-cover, coop* and *co-op, overage* and *over-age, reform* and *re-form*.

62-b Word Division

Hyphens are used to link parts of a word divided between lines of text. Canadian practice regarding word breaks is to follow the pronunciation by dividing between syllables. (The entries in most dictionaries indicate the syllable breaks in words.)

Job-Related Writing

Part XII is available online at
www.nelson.com/site/cdnwriterspocketguide5e.

This section covers

- memos and e-mails
- formal letters
- reports

Also available on the companion site are Test
Yourself questions and a variety of other resources
related to writing. This section is included in the
index that follows; the page numbers for entries
that appear in Part XII are preceded by the letter *W*.

ACKNOWLEDGMENTS

We must begin by acknowledging the many colleagues and the fourteen thousand students in Quebec, Ontario, Manitoba, Alberta, and British Columbia who taught us much of what we know about writing and writing instruction.

The Nelson Education team has been an essential part of developing the book. We particularly want to acknowledge Laura Macleod, Lisa Berland, Claire Horsnell, Lisa Laframboise, Pushpa, Loretta Lee, Peter Papayanakis, and Johanna Liburd.

Our thanks also go to two of our librarians at Kwantlen, Jean McKendry and Jan Penhorwood, who were essential in guiding us through the significant changes that have occurred in online research. The entry of discovery layers and the Summon Search aid, and the creation of regional alliances in postsecondary libraries have made student research very different than it was even six to eight years ago.

It is evident that these search aids give students expanded access to resources beyond the capacity of a single library. The nature of publishing and distributing books and journals continues to change and reshape research and academic writing. We would also like to thank Paul Tyndall, chair of the English Department, Kwantlen Polytechnic University, for helping us find a new MLA-style sample essay for this edition.

Thanks go to our daughters, Genevieve, Signe, and Loa, who reviewed the text and helped keep us current in our examples and our understanding of online developments. It is still a pleasure to say that this text is the product of two generations of Finnbogason-Valleau thought.

Thanks to Yit Shang for allowing us to dominate the dining room with the piles of paper that always accumulate during the process of updating a text. Finally, we would like to dedicate this book to the memory of Marsha, whose spirit helped guide us and keep us on task, and whose common sense and humanity continues to permeate our writing.

INDEX

Note: Page numbers prefixed with "W" refer to web content.